A MAN OF MY WORD

a memoir

BEATON TULK

with Laurie Blackwood Pike

FLANKER PRESS LIMITED
ST. JOHN'S

Beaton Tulk

Library and Archives Canada Cataloguing in Publication

Tulk, Beaton, 1944-, author
    A man of my word : a memoir / Beaton Tulk with Laurie Blackwood Pike.

Includes index.
Issued in print and electronic formats.
ISBN 978-1-77117-670-5 (softcover).--ISBN 978-1-77117-671-2 (EPUB).--
ISBN 978-1-77117-672-9 (Kindle).--ISBN 978-1-77117-673-6 (PDF)

    1. Tulk, Beaton, 1944-. 2. Premiers (Canada)--Newfoundland and
Labrador--Biography. 3. Politicians--Newfoundland and Labrador--Biography.
4. Newfoundland and Labrador--Politics and government--1989-2003.
I. Pike, Laurie Blackwood, 1944-, author II. Title.

FC2177.1.T85A3 2018   971.8'05092   C2018-901650-7
                                         C2018-901651-5

PRINTED IN CANADA

MIX
Paper from
responsible sources
FSC® C016245

This paper has been certified to meet the environmental and social standards of the Forest Stewardship Council® (FSC®) and comes from responsibly managed forests, and verified recycled sources.

Cover design by Graham Blair

FLANKER PRESS LTD.
PO BOX 2522, STATION C
ST. JOHN'S, NL
CANADA

TELEPHONE: (709) 739-4477   FAX: (709) 739-4420   TOLL-FREE: 1-866-739-4420

WWW.FLANKERPRESS.COM

9 8 7 6 5 4 3 2 1

Canada

Canada Council   Conseil des Arts
for the Arts   du Canada

Newfoundland
Labrador

We acknowledge the financial support of the Government of Canada through the Canada Book Fund (CBF) and the Government of Newfoundland and Labrador, Department of Tourism, Culture, Industry and Innovation for our publishing activities. We acknowledge the support of the Canada Council for the Arts, which last year invested $157 million to bring the arts to Canadians throughout the country. *Nous remercions le Conseil des arts du Canada de son soutien. L'an dernier, le Conseil a investi 157 millions de dollars pour mettre de l'art dans la vie des Canadiennes et des Canadiens de tout le pays.*

Dedication

First, I want to express my appreciation to Laurie Blackwood Pike (a.k.a. Grandpa Pike) for undertaking this venture with me. With the way I "talks," I know it was not easy listening to the tapes he used to interview and organize my rambling ways. Thanks, Laurie.

I will forever be indebted to the wonderful owners at Flanker Press—Garry, Margo, and their son Jerry—for taking the chance that enough people would want to read this book to make it worthwhile. They are tremendous people.

Both my father and mother's people were of "good stock." Benjamin and Minnie Tulk, and Francis and Edith West worked hard to raise their families and taught them the value of hard work, community, and charity. My father's parents raised three sons: my father, Japhet, and my uncles Enos and Beaton. Because of his war service and his personality, Uncle Beaton was the hero of all the family. Uncle Enos was my next-door neighbour for years and became one of the best friends and supporters I ever had. He loved his fun, playing jokes on me, and was the best card player I ever met. I loved him dearly, and he died too early at age seventy-one from cancer. I cannot say enough about their families. Joan, Yvonne, John, Barry, Pauline, Brenda, Beverley, Bert, Boyd and Brad, Aunt Louise,

Aunt Leah. In the case of my mother, her sisters Aunt Lillian, Aunt Hilda (still living at age ninety), and Aunt Ethel and their children Jean Coles, Dorothy, and Ronald Dawe—I have great respect for all of them. They have all carried on the tradition of hard work and kindness inherited from their ancestors. I hope to write the story of my family so that their ancestors can know who they were and point out a few stories about them. That will be a family effort comprised, I hope, of their stories.

When I married Dora in 1996, I became part of the family of Otto and Amy Skiffington. Otto and my father were the same kind of people—hard-working and loving their family. Besides being a lumberman who my father met in Millertown, Otto did mixed farming. When I look at his farmland and hear from my brother-in-law about the stones he removed, I can only marvel at his determination.

Amy is another story. A lady whom everyone in her family and community loved, and she them. I knew her for only a few years and have often said, "I loved my mother dearly, but if you asked me to choose between them, it would be an impossible task."

Otto and Amy had eleven children: Mary, who died as a baby, Boyd (Phyllis), Amelia (Dave), Don (Ann), Bernice (Gus), Dora (Beaton), Doug, who was killed by a car at the age of seventeen, Dorothy (Boyce), Alliston (Jim), Lee (Harvey), and Sandra (Brendon, "Skip"). They are a unique family who will defend their siblings to the death and never end a telephone call or leave a gathering without using the words "I love you." It has taught me a lot about being close and to use these same words. Since Boyce's death, Dorothy lives with Dora and me, making me feel a little like Jack Tripper (I could not resist).

Along with every member of my family, I want to thank every one of them for the journey that my life has been so far. I have been truly blessed.

Contents

Beaton and Dora Tulk

Introduction

This is Beaton's book, make no mistake. It is written in the first person, and that which follows, after his introduction, is his story. I have known Beaton since 1979. At the time Beaton was MHA for Fogo. We did some business together in the early 1980s and got to know each other well.

We spent many evenings in his room or mine at the Albatross and other hotels in Gander going over business plans, pro forma, budgets, and discussing subjects as diverse and important as history, politics, religion, and good beer. I remember one evening in particular when we were at the Hotel Gander, I believe it was, doing some practical evaluation of beer and discussing politics. I told him he should seek the leadership of his party. He laughed.

"Never," he told me. "I have no interest." I would have quit my job in a minute and worked with him on a campaign, helped write speeches—not that he needed help—been a personal assistant, or done anything else the man wanted. Beaton Tulk had a special way with people that made you like him instantly. I believed he could win and, if he won, become the next premier.

I was not a starstruck kid. We were the same age—thirty-four—so of course we still are, now in our seventies, although he promises to win that contest by double digits. I saw Beaton only occasionally over the next number of years, but I followed his career. Beaton didn't seek the leadership at that upcoming convention—or ever. Leadership sought him. He was voted unanimously, by his peers, to be leader of the Newfoundland and Labrador Liberal Party in 2000, when Premier Brian Tobin resigned to go to Ottawa. Beaton was sworn in as premier on October 16 of 2000.

Some months ago Beaton and I met for breakfast at Cora's in St. John's, and he told me an anecdote from his childhood. That story, plain and simple, explained perfectly to me where he came from. I suggested that he start his book with that anecdote. The upbringing that he had, I believe, helped make him successful in his later careers in education, politics, business, and public service.

Beaton starts on the next page, with the story he told me after I asked the Cora's waiter for marmalade.

Grandpa Pike
March 2018

1

Childhood

MY DAD

I was sitting at the breakfast table with my parents, who were living with me, when my seventy-eight-year-old father casually said, "Pass the marmalade." I reached to hand it to him but stopped mid-pass, having a childhood flashback.

"You hate marmalade, Dad."

"No, he loves marmalade," my mother said quickly, answering for him.

"But you wouldn't touch it when I was a youngster. You said you hated it," I told him.

My dad stayed quiet, and again my mother spoke. "He only said that so there would be more for you guys."

As children we never went to bed hungry, and even in the worst winters, my sister, Blanche, and I were never cold at night. I assure you, though, there were few luxuries, and even less marmalade.

He was named Japhet Ronald Tulk, but everyone called him Japh. My dad worked hard and earned way more than he was ever paid. A slight man, probably not over five foot six or five foot seven, he could hold his own, and then some, in the Millertown pulpwoods. A lumberjack and at times a teamster, if he had to shoe one of those heavy draft horses, the horse knew who was in charge.

Tough as a tiger when he needed to be, he was as gentle as a kitten with me and my sister. He'd never raise his hand to me, let alone give me a good thrashing, which, at times, I richly deserved. "Spare the rod and spoil the child" may have been a common sentiment at the time, but he took a more enlightened approach to discipline. A father should be the model to which a son aspires. I'm proud of the example he set. I hope I haven't let him down too badly.

Dad started work when he was fourteen. He worked for the Anglo-Newfoundland Development (A.N.D.) Company for nineteen years. After that he got into running freight and passenger boats out of Lewisporte—my uncle did that, too. Later he operated a truck and a J5— a snow tractor, on tracks like a snowmobile. You could go anywhere with them. He hauled wood and anything else that needed hauling. Finally, he started working with the engineers at the Department of Highways, and he stayed there until he retired. He also had his own sawmill at one point.

He came close to beating me, only once—or at least I think he came close. That happened one Easter Sunday after church. My mother and I usually sat in the balcony. I snuck down below to the back of the church, where my mother couldn't see me, and sat with a bunch of my friends. An Easter pageant was in progress, and some of the girls were doing readings. I made faces at these young ladies to get them laughing.

The gentleman running the pageant didn't name me in church, but he said that someone down back was creating a disturbance. My mother knew instinctively who it was. She met me on the front steps afterwards and said, "It was you, right?" I admitted it.

When we got home and Dad found out, all he said was, "Beaton! Leave this house for a couple of hours. If not, I don't know what I'll do with you." I got out quickly. He meant it.

He was a pleasant man almost all the time. I can't say anything bad about him. Smart. Good with math. He could add up a half-dozen three-digit numbers in his head. He worked, as I said earlier, for A.N.D. at

Millertown, and he was still there, in the woods, during the Badger riot in 1959. It was legalized slavery, so it was.

If we were ever tempted to feel sorry for ourselves back in Ladle Cove, all we had to do was think of Dad, working sun-up to sunset with a bucksaw, a long way from his family—flies and heat in the summer, and bitter cold in winter. Especially so in the early years, sleeping on a bed of tree boughs, and for heat only a Grand Falls blanket (a rough khaki-coloured blanket supplied by A.N.D.) and a stove that burnt out in the middle of the night. Dozens of smelly men in the same room, snoring, coughing, and sleeping in their day clothes to keep warm.

They were paid ninety cents a cord. Ninety bloody cents! The first ninety cents each day went for room and board—the board being mostly pork and beans. I've already described the room part of the deal. It took the best part of four hours in good weather to cut and stack a cord of pulpwood with only a bucksaw. We treated prisoners of war better.

Newfoundlanders survived in those times by growing and raising everything they could for themselves, trading things, cutting their own firewood, etc. Not many had two coins to rub together, let alone folding money.

My grandfather was a fisherman, and after he sold his fifty or 100 quintals of fish—whatever it was—and got his gear for the next season, he might have had three or four dollars to put in his pocket—for a year's work!

My dad worked tirelessly when he was home as well, but most of the responsibilities there were left to my mother—with help from the youngsters.

MY MOTHER

My mother's people came from a little community nearby called White Point. There were only five or six families there. The community died out and most people relocated to Ladle Cove. Her father put the house on skids and moved it over the bog to the cove. They attached rope to the skids and tied an anchor to the other end. The anchor was carried ahead until the rope was taut, and then they set the anchor down into the bog until she caught. Then, using a block and tackle, they dragged the house to the anchor.

Next the anchor was carried ahead, fixed again into the bog, and the process repeated until they made the few miles to Ladle Cove.

She was named Sadie Mariah West at birth. She was tall, about five foot ten, I'd say, a slim, fine-looking woman with dark hair. She put on a bit of weight in her later years—like many of us do. Mom knew who she was, and she was comfortable in her own skin.

Religious, she went to church every Sunday and loved to sing. You could hear her voice, clear as a bell, above all the other voices, from anywhere in the building. We were United Church at that time. The church had been Methodist until several different denominations joined together in 1925 to form the United Church of Canada. There were no other churches at that time in Ladle Cove. I didn't even meet a Roman Catholic until I went away to university.

She didn't work outside the home, but there was plenty to do there. In addition to cooking, cleaning, looking after us, tending the garden, milking the goats, knitting, darning, and all the other things a mother did, she sewed. She was a very good seamstress. One December she made sixteen winter coats, for "her own" and others in the community. I still remember crawling around as a young child under that old treadle-powered Singer sewing machine, playing in the scraps of cloth and thread on the floor.

She kept a good home, sweeping, dusting, mopping, and polishing the old cast-iron Comfort stove with "stove black." Later we got a shiny chrome or nickel range, but Dad complained the "damn thing" didn't give off the same heat. He'd never convince Mom to go back to the old stove, though.

And he'd never take the range or anything else that Mom wanted or liked out of the house. She'd tell him he was too old-fashioned. His words were always, "If it makes her happy, that's it."

She wasn't a gossip and couldn't abide anyone else gossiping. There was a group of married women at our house one night talking about so many young girls getting pregnant those days. Her reply was, "If every bird fell that was shot at, there wouldn't be many birds flying," implying, of course, that they weren't bad because they got pregnant, but just unlucky.

When someone would criticize another person, she'd say, "Let every barrel stand on its own bottom," which meant let people live their own lives. If I did something wrong, she knew it intuitively, and I got punished but was never beaten.

If I was accused wrongly of doing something bad, she was like a mother bear defending her cubs. I remember a kid goat getting drowned in the community, and I was accused of doing it. I hadn't been involved, and Mom knew I hadn't because I had been with her the whole time it happened. When buddy started complaining about it and named me, she told him, "He didn't do it. I have a kid goat, and it's yours if you can prove that my son drowned yours." The man didn't get her kid, but I think she "got his goat."

She never drank alcohol, never swore, and never smoked. My mom died of cancer at age seventy-one.

Just to show where I probably got some of my impish nature, I feel compelled to tell this story about my maternal grandmother, Edith. She was as impish as they come. Where the divisions ended and started I do not know, but Ladle Cove was known to have a downharbour, a middle, and southern (sudder) side. The road ran around a pond. We lived downharbour, my grandmother in the middle, and the school was on the southern side. As Roland Dawe, her other grandson, lived on Fogo Island, I was the only grandson around, so on many a day I went to her house for lunch.

One particular day when I arrived, she was grinning from ear to ear. She said, "Your grandfather has a new hearing aid. I don't believe that works." My grandfather was, as we used to say, deaf as a block. Their house had what we called a back kitchen, really a porch with two doors opposite each other.

She said, "He's up by the barn. Lets see if he can hear you." Out we go to the back kitchen. She stayed behind me as I said in a normal voice, "Frank." No reply. Then a little louder: "Frank." Again, no reply.

Meanwhile, she was behind me saying, "I knew it, I knew it! But try a little louder." Then I roared out, "Frank!" Back came the reply: "I hears ya, ya whore's son!" Now, if you had called my mother that particular word, he would have made mincemeat out of you. In the meantime, Grandmother, who was as big around as she was tall, was on her hands and knees, shaking with laughter and saying, "Upon my soul to God, it works!"

At that time, hearing aids were run by a battery large enough that it had to be stored in your shirt pocket with a cord going up to the receiver. Of course, when you were not using it you turned it down to save the battery. When you turned it up too high there would be nothing, only a squawk. My impish grandmother would sit across the kitchen and move her lips without saying a word. Grandfather would turn the hearing up a notch. Again the movement of her lips, and again he'd turn it up. After a couple of more times the squawk would come and he would clasp his two hands over his ears. Then with a grin she would turn her attention to something else. She'd had her bit of fun.

CHORES

Filling the woodbox and the water barrel was a daily chore—as was feeding and watering the hens, which we called "coupies." We had a well, but like many others there, it ran dry in the summer. We hauled up what we needed from Uncle George's well. No pump—we drew it up by bucket and rope and carried it back to our place.

My earliest memory is of going in the woods with my father to cut firewood when he was home from Millertown. Gone for months at a time, his main job when home was to make sure we had enough firewood to last during the time he'd be gone again, and to bring home the paltry wages he made in those days in the lumberwoods.

My mother had a large vegetable garden. We grew cabbage, carrots, potatoes, parsnips, and turnip. We hauled capelin up from the beach to fertilize the garden, and we transported water for the animals and the house. In the summer we hoed and weeded the garden. We snared rabbits and the odd fox in the wintertime. We ate the rabbits, but we sold the pelts from any fox we got to Sydney I. Robinson Furs in Winnipeg.

When I was about eight, I got a horse—a pony, I suppose you'd say, but either way, June was mine! I had a dog, too, named King. He was big, about fifty pounds, with long brown hair. Water dogs, we called them then. They'd go into the water to retrieve ducks for you when you were hunting. My mother kept the goats for milk. It was my job to get them into the pen to milk, and she'd milk them.

When the chores were all done, we had supper. After that, in the wintertime, it was time to study. Mom polished the chimney of the kerosene oil lamp and trimmed the wick to provide maximum light to study at the kitchen table.

My mother did more than anyone to impress upon me the importance of getting a good education. That, to her, would be the difference in my having a good life or a lifelong struggle. Every night her words were, "Learn your lessons, my son, get an education, get a good job—not like your father, having to work in the woods, or your grandfather at the fish."

At that time her idea of getting a good job was to be become a teacher, get a government job, or become a minister. I got all three, but as everybody can guess, I never became the type of minister that she meant. I suspect that she probably knew it wasn't going to happen anyway.

After supper it was time to go out with my friends and try to find some deviltry to get into.

I was born on May 22, 1944, in my parents' house in Ladle Cove, and my grandmother was midwife. A small baby, they didn't expect me to survive. I was wrapped in toile cloth and put under the Comfort stove to keep me warm. Obviously I survived, but I grew slowly, and there was no size to me at all until I was twelve or fourteen years old. We lived in a bungalow until I was about six, when Dad built us a house up behind it. Actually, he built—or almost built—two.

He had someone else start the first one, but when he went to frame it up, he found it was about six inches off square, so he abandoned it and then built another.

When I was six years old, my sister, Blanche, married a young man in the community, Sandy West, so she was only in the new house with us for a short time. The occupants now consisted of me and my parents after Blanche went off to start her own family.

Blanche was smart. Ten times smarter than me, she could sit down and write you a poem in minutes—with words that made sense and with the rhyme and rhythm right. Her spelling was perfect—not a single mistake all through school. I know this for a fact because she left all her scribblers and school papers when she moved out. I'd read them, and it made me feel closer to her after she left.

I loved Blanche. She was a wonderful big sister to me. One of my most treasured pictures is of her pushing me across the pond on an old sled and in coats made by my mother. I only wish she could have gotten what she deserved out of life.

The second house was a two-storey, five-bedroom house, properly built and the walls insulated with old clothing—one of the best houses in Ladle Cove. This house was to be passed on to me and would have room enough for a large family. I've always believed that my parents had only two children because they were not sure that they could provide for more. They planned to somehow get me a proper education so I could get a good job, not have to work as hard as my dad, and be able to raise a large family.

LADLE COVE

Ladle Cove is a community on the northeast coast of Newfoundland and Labrador and at its biggest had a population of 225–250. It had good soil for growing vegetable and grass for horses, cows, goats, and sheep. This was a godsend during those hard times. How could you go hungry if you were willing to work? And the people of Ladle Cove did not mind working.

The first permanent settler came to Ladle Cove in 1862. My family arrived somewhere around 1870 from Newtown, which is now part of New-Wes-Valley. Ladle Cove offered good access to the fishing grounds and fertile land for growing vegetables and keeping farm animals.

The early settlers took full advantage of the location. By the 1880s, surplus farm produce was being shipped to several communities to the west. We were considered a model outport, and during the Great Depression of the 1930s we had the second-lowest incidence of "relief" recipients in the whole province.

On the north side of Ladle Cove we had very shallow water. We used to say when the water fell—or when the tide was out—that a flatfish would sunburn. Not much water, eh? The south side had a little deeper water but no more shelter from storms than the north side.

When we had a storm, usually in fall and winter, our shoreline would be pounded by fifteen-foot white-crested waves.

In spite of the breastwork constructed by the local road board, the power of the waves would still drive water onto our roads.

On many occasions our fishermen watched their wharves float out the harbour or wash ashore. They would salvage what they could, but a great deal washed out to sea. Heartbreaking, to say the least, but by spring they were ready to go again.

Ladle Cove was a beautiful place to grow up in, especially in summer. When I see the dangers that children are challenged with today, I feel like I grew up in a cocoon—protected by that community and its people.

There were no roads leading in or out of Ladle Cove in those days. You went outside the community by boat or by horse or foot overland. Earlier they had used dog teams in the winter, but I think the last of them was gone when I was four or five.

We had two stores in this outport of about 200 people: the Fishermen's Union Trading Company down on the wharf; and another store operated by Jacob Pinsent. Uncle Jake's, we called it. Later on, Edward West and Arthur Wellon were in business as well. There was also a school, the church, and the Orange Lodge. There was no library, restaurant, garage, or other such modern places to hang out, but we found enough to do without them.

You could get basic patent medicines at the two stores, usually Gerald S. Doyle Products in a blue glass bottle, but there was no doctor, dentist, or clinic.

We had a nurse, though—the finest kind. She lived in Musgrave Harbour, an English girl who had married a local man, Walter Cuff, from that community. Nurse Cuff, as she was known, was absolutely revered in Ladle Cove. She could do anything a doctor could do. She was twenty-five or thirty then, I suppose. She'd walk overland in winter the five or six miles through the woods, mud, snow, and ice to come see us.

I was the Government House Leader when we put licensed practical nurses in place in the health care system. It was with great pride that I got to stand in the House of Assembly and name her the first LPN in Newfoundland. An exceptional woman for her time—or any time.

DEVILTRY

Mostly it was not evil stuff, just pranks and practical jokes, although I did get in one bit of trouble that I felt truly sorry for later. I'll get that out of the way first.

Ladle Cove was very shallow. As we would say, a flatfish would sunburn when the tide was out. Therefore, bigger supply boats had to anchor off and reload onto a smaller vessel to bring the freight ashore. One day we were helping Uncle Jake get his goods ashore when my friend Wilson West and I decided to steal a box of Coffee Crisp bars. We hid it up in the woods and ate away at the bars until another kid found out, and we had to let him in on it, too.

The success of this enterprise emboldened us, and next time we stole a case of Del Monte canned peaches. We pushed them in the wharf, but a guy on the beach, David West, spotted us and we were busted.

When I got home that evening, there were no cops, but every authority in the community was there. The minister, and Uncle Jake, the teacher, and my mother launched into what you would now call an intervention. By the time they were finished with me, I was ashamed for stealing what wasn't mine. I never, ever stole anything again.

After that, I couldn't even pick up a penny off the floor without turning it in—much less anything of significant value.

The rest of the evil I got into was minor by comparison. For example, if a crowd of young fellows was coming over from Aspen Cove, my buddy Wilson and I and some other kids would meet them with a barrage of rocks. The girls were ours, even if they didn't want us, and someone had to protect them, right?

With no place for the teenagers to get together, away from the adults, they took to getting together at one house, a different one each weekend, and having a scoff. This would be in the earlier part of the evening, and later they'd break up into pairs or foursomes and do what teenagers are wont to do.

When I was younger, the boys my age would prank them. One of the things we'd do was sneak up on that "party house" and find a way to disrupt their festivities.

One night while the b'ys hid in the bushes keeping watch, I got up on the roof and placed a nice solid sod over the chimney. It wasn't long before the house filled with smoke and the teens came pouring out. Then we snuck in, stole the scoff pot off the stove, and hid it up in the woods.

Minor stuff, really. In such a small community, people were going to find out eventually who did what, and we were all in it together anyway, so nothing cruel or really harmful was done. There were no murders or suicides in my time there.

No robberies, no attempted robberies—unless you count those delicious Coffee Crisps. And that case of canned peaches, which we never even got to taste.

READING AND LISTENING

I got my love of reading from my father's side of the family. I loved it—and I'd read anything, from the instructions on a box of Rinso to my Bible—the latter which my mother gave me for passing grade four. There was no bookstore, no public library, and of course it was long before the Internet.

Gosling Memorial Library in St. John's used to send books to our school in grey wooden boxes. There were usually forty or fifty books, at various reading levels, per box. It didn't take long for me to devour any that were up to and past my reading level.

One shipment arrived in the fall, and once I'd read all I could, or wanted to, I had to wait till the spring shipment. That came when the first coastal boat or steamer arrived after the pack ice was well off shore.

I also had access to the *Sunday Herald*, the forerunner of the *Newfoundland Herald*, then owned by Don Jamieson and Geoff Sterling. In addition, there were usually copies of the *Free Press Weekly* and the monthly *Family Herald*.

Maybe I was blessed. With no TV then, we had no cartoon shows where the coyote tried to drop the Acme anvil down on the Road Runner's head, violent movies, sex flicks, or PlayStations with war games—and then again, perhaps I was not blessed. I had a clear mind, but maybe it was too clear.

Maybe we were too protected then. I believe I could have benefited greatly from the free flow of information we have today. But as my mother might have said, "Who knows, my child?"

One book, though, was always available—the King James version of the Bible, which, as I said, my mother had given me. I kept it on my nightstand. I read the stories about Creation, the Great Flood, Jonah and the Whale, and the battles fought by the mighty kings in the Old Testament.

The New Testament was something else again—especially the central character, Jesus. Every house in our community had a picture of Jesus hanging on the wall. The most popular was the one where he is kneeling, dressed in a long white robe, gazing skyward in prayerful supplication to God. He had long hair—like Elvis Presley, but even longer.

Elvis was taboo in this 1950s community. When I wanted to grow my hair long, I compared the two, Jesus and the Presley guy, hoping to get my mother's permission.

Instead she got angry and, in a voice reserved for my worst transgressions, said, "How can you compare that sinner to our Saviour?

The devil will have you, unless you ask forgiveness!" That didn't make sense to me.

My mother was sinless, in my mind, yet she was always praying and asking forgiveness of the Lord. My father, on the other hand, would swear like a trooper when he was frustrated. When my mother would admonish him, he'd simply reply, "I'm only relieving my god---- mind."

I kept reading my Bible, though, and especially the red-letter parts of the New Testament—the words of Christ.

We had a battery-operated radio, powered by an Eveready dry cell. A new battery in the fall had to last until spring, so we used the radio sparingly. Mom would take the battery and wrap it in a blanket at night so it wouldn't get cold, then unwrap it again in the morning after the house had warmed up. When it was down to the last dregs of power, sometimes my dad would put it on a cooler part of the hot stove. Once the battery heated up, it would last for a while more.

We listened regularly to the *Gerald S. Doyle News Bulletin*. Excluding hospital reports on outport people in St. John's hospitals, the coastal boat schedule, the weather, and advertising of Doyle company products, the news lasted about ten minutes per night.

So, yes, we got to listen to the news, *The Big Six* (an Irish music program), and on Sunday mornings, Sunday gospel hymns.

My mother knew the words and music to all of these hymns, and her strong voice, singing along, was often the first thing I heard Sunday morning as I lay in my bed.

Sometimes at night we'd get a radio station that came in on the skip, from Antigonish, Nova Scotia. From my little world in Ladle Cove, that might be like New York or Florida is to today's youngsters. CJFX 580 AM, in Antigonish, went on the air in 1943, broadcasting with 1,000 watts power.

It was a variety-format station, and in the 1950s it broadcast rock 'n' roll, country and western, and Celtic music—along with news, weather, and sports.

The odd time when my parents were out I'd disobey and turn on the radio. They always knew. Maybe they could tell by the warmth of the radio, which heated up with all those tubes inside it.

I don't know for sure how, but they always knew. Perhaps I had been practising my Elvis moves to "Jailhouse Rock" on CJFX and was still flushed and out of breath when they got home.

SPORTS AND GAMES

We had fun outdoors, too. We played a game similar to baseball, we played soccer, and we skated on the pond in the middle of our community. We had the old strap-on blades that you'd attach to the soles of your boots, and there were a few modern skates as well. We played hockey, and for a puck we'd use the heel of an old boot, a small knot of wood, or even a frozen chunk of horse manure.

We made our own hockey sticks from "crannicks." These were the twisted stems and roots of dead or weathered spruce or fir trees. They were tough, and many of them had the natural angle for the blade. Some people called them "crunnicks" or "cronnicks," and people from other places referred to these short, tough trees as "tuckamore." Older people also used them to make a strong walking stick or cane. We employed them more to beat the legs out from under another player, "by accident," of course, when they got the puck.

I became a very good hockey player by age sixteen or seventeen. I was twenty, however, before I got my first good pair of hockey skates—Tackaberrys by CCM. Mine were Tack 1. They cost $150 at that time.

Another game we played a lot was tiddely, known in other communities by a variety of other names, like flick stick, kit kat, or piddely. It wasn't a complicated game, and the object was to flick a short stick as far as you could with a longer stick.

Then the one "at bat" placed the longer stick where the shorter stick had rested—across two stones or junks of wood. The fielder closest to where the short stick landed then got one chance to knock the longer stick off its perch. The rules were different by bay, and often by community. If anyone wants to learn to play it, there are good descriptions on the Internet or in *The Flanker Dictionary of Newfoundland English*.

I had no childhood heroes in the traditional sense. There were no

TV or movies, so to us there was no *Superman* or *Lone Ranger and Tonto*. The heroes respected by all in our community were the war heroes—older men who went overseas to war and came back.

There was Beaton Tulk, the uncle for whom I am named. He was away when I was born, and I was named for him—in case he didn't make it back. There were Simon Tulk, Wes Stratton, Ronald West, Baxter West, and a few others. The ones who weren't respected were those who could have gone but hadn't—single men or men with no families and no important job to do here. My first hero in the modern sense was the great Gordie Howe.

When I was about ten years old, my father bought me a yearling pony. To me, June was a beautiful pony. She grew to about 500 or 600 pounds and was coal black, with white "stockings" and a star on her forehead. I never rode her, bareback or saddled, but I drove her in a slide or a cart.

We used her to bring up capelin off the beach for fertilizer and for hauling out firewood. June always brings back a flood of memories. I suppose that's like today when a young person gets their driver's licence or their first car. I recall one particular Sunday when I was twelve as clearly as if it happened yesterday. Here's how I remember it.

I didn't have to get up early on a Sunday. I laid in bed reading the Bible or some other book after I woke up, until I heard Uncle Will's footsteps crunching the snow on our bridge on his way to visit Dad, where they would "solve the world's problems." I listened in.

They talked about Jack Pickersgill, Joey Smallwood, the price of wheat on the prairies, labour unrest at Millertown, and the possibility of a fall election. There was no church this morning, as the weather was too rough for the minister to get in from Musgrave Harbour.

I started to smell the wonderful flavours of boiled cabbage, carrot, turnip, pease pudding, molasses pudding, and the roast moose and duck which would be our dinner. That was the signal for me to get up, so on went my shirt, socks, and breeks.

As the clock struck twelve, Uncle Will got up to leave, speculating that his dinner would be on the table—time he got home. While Mom made the gravy, I negotiated with Dad for the use of the pony and slide later that day.

My plan was to take my friends for a ride and to show off a little. Dad had bought June as a yearling two years ago, and now, as a three-year-old mare, it was time for me to be working with her regularly.

He was reluctant for me to take her out alone, as she was still not properly broken in yet. He was afraid that after resting all winter, out of harness, she might be too much for a young boy to handle. Also, he didn't want me "teaching" her bad habits which might be hard for him to correct later.

Then Mom piped in. "He'll be killed with that horse yet. I don't know why you bought it for him—he's only twelve years old, you know!" But Dad was ready for her objection. "Sadie, my maid, I was teaming horses when I was only three years older than him. Sure, he can handle one small horse like that if he stays on the pond."

Mom relented, but only after Dad agreed that I would attend Sunday school every Sunday. I suppose she thought that, if I got killed, church would ensure that I'd go to a better place. Dad readily agreed, I reluctantly agreed, and the deal was sealed.

I guarantee you that I was the happiest kid in any bay as I dug into that hot Sunday dinner. I gulped my meal in great forkfuls, leaving barely a toothmark in much of it, I'm sure. I was thinking of Missy, a girl who normally wouldn't give me the time of day.

I planned to charge the other kids for a ride and keep her waiting. Finally, she'd beg me for a ride on the horse and slide, and I'd relent.

As I was leaving the table, Mom spoke up.

"Haven't you forgot something?"

"Yes. Thank You, Lord," I replied.

"That too," said Mom, laughing, "but I was thinking of dessert."

As I sat back down to eat my caramel tart dessert, Dad spoke up.

"While your mother gets ready to take you to Sunday school, I'll help you tackle the horse. Then all will be ready when you get back."

I gulped that dessert like someone was trying to steal it. Dad savoured each spoonful slowly, and I was thinking that if we were going to cut grass, and I had to help him, I bet he'd eat a lot faster. Finally, he was done, and we dressed warmly and headed out to the barn.

Dad opened the big barn doors. The frozen hinges creaked from the frosty night, and as we entered the dimly lit interior, I said, "Dad, I know how to harness her."

I'd watched him do it many times before. Dad stood, ready to assist as I methodically harnessed June from memory. Horses, like anything else, don't like to be bound tight, and most will give you trouble with the girth strap—which holds the harness in place. Many horses will inflate their belly or chest area as you tighten this strap. I suppose they do it by holding their breath or flexing their muscles. I hadn't learned that yet.

Dad instructed me to tighten it more so the harness wouldn't slide around later. We left the bridle for after Sunday school but kept her halter on and tied her back in the stall. I felt about six inches taller as we walked back to the house.

I'd harnessed the horse with very little guidance from Dad, and I'd learned that thing about the girth strap in the process. I think my dad was proud, too.

Now it seemed like forever waiting for my mother to get ready for Sunday school. It was easy to forget that she had spent the time that we were in the barn cleaning up from dinner and doing the dishes. Finally, she put on her hat, Sunday coat, and furtops—boots with a fringe of fur around the top—and was ready to go.

By the time Mom got to the church, I was a full seven minutes ahead of her—enough time to tell everyone I would have the horse and slide later. I didn't hear a word in Sunday school that day, and as soon as the superintendent gave the benediction, I had my cap and mitts on and was out the door.

I ran for home and the barn, leaving Mom to walk back alone. In the barn, Dad already had the bridle and bit on, and June was ready for the shafts of the slide.

The slide was known as a sleigh elsewhere, but since it's designed to slide, that's probably a more apt name. (If she won't slide, then there ain't no ice or snow, and you should be using a cart or buggy.) Getting a horse "in the shafts" can be a tricky process, and Dad took over. The worst can happen and the horse step on a shaft, breaking it, and it would take a long time to even jury-rig a broken one, let alone make a new one.

Dad loaded me up with instructions and cautions, and although he was smiling when I finally hollered, "Giddap, giddap!" I'm sure he must have looked worried as I pulled out of sight.

We were at the pond, where I was going to give rides to my friends—for a price—in what seemed like seconds.

June was still jumpy and full of energy. I knew I had to wear her down a little before taking anyone aboard. The last thing I needed was to lose control of her and have to face the taunting at school the next day. I took her down the windswept pond, and as we approached the end, she wanted to go straight out the other end on the well-worn path.

I pulled so hard on the right rein that June's nose was practically facing me. She had no choice. She came off the path and into about eighteen inches of snow, and I held the rein tight until we were running in the deep snow parallel to the sled road back toward the crowd.

I kept her in the snow, and she worked for her supper. After a couple times around the pond pulling through that deep snow, I wore her down and she started to understand who the boss was. As I brought her to a quiet stop by my friends, they all clamoured to get aboard.

Now there was just the minor matter of them pledging their fare. They pledged recesses—special treats from their lunch bags—and other goodies until I had enough for a month. I sorted my "customers" into pairs, as that's all we could safely handle per ride. I purposely left Missy for last—even though she had pledged two chocolate bars and a bag of chips. A couple of guys would have pledged the same thing, along with their soul to the devil, for a ride alone with her.

The other guys believed I wanted to put her in her place for being "haughty," and that's why I'd taken her last. To me she was the most beautiful creature God had ever put breath to, and I wanted her alone.

She sat quietly but with a smile on her face, and as we were coming around the pond the second time, she said, "Why did you leave me until last, alone?"

"It just happened that way," I mumbled, trying to sound casual.

With that, she put her innocent smile back on and asked, "Why are you giving me two rides in one?"

"Because you were the last one," I muttered, and then emboldened by her closeness and obvious appreciation of the extra-long ride, I added, "And I wanted to ask you to the teenage dance at the Orange Lodge next Saturday, and . . . and . . . you don't have to give me the bars and chips either!"

I almost let go of the reins, and I suppose my face went red when she replied, "Of course. I'd be glad to be your date." I had no idea that her decision had nothing to do with me, but rather the chocolate bars and chips. I'd find that out later, but for now my joy was overwhelming.

If my head and heart had felt any lighter after I helped her down out of the seat, I could have taken the horse and sleigh right through the air on the way back to the barn. My twelve-year-old heart was pounding in my chest, like my grandfather's old make-and-break eight-horsepower Acadia boat engine.

Years later, when we had gone our separate ways, Missy, whenever she got the chance, would say to me, "It just happened that way, eh Beaton?"

The date didn't go nearly as well as the sleigh ride, and I didn't even see it coming. The dance was chaperoned by the Orangemen and their wives as a community service for teenagers. You could bring a date, but the hall was strictly guarded against any hanky-panky.

Even though we had no television, there were records, and they were played on a manual wind-up record player. Some of the girls had pictures of Elvis, but his music would not be played at the dance because every adult in the community believed he was nothing but a source of corruption for young people.

The best we could hope for, to hear Elvis, was to sneak a scattered listen on the old battery radio when our parents were out playing Flinch at someone's house. Flinch is an old-fashioned Parker Brothers card game. Missy had told me that I should wear my hair like Elvis and promised to get me some Brylcreem to hold it in place.

The word was out that Missy was my date for the dance, provided I wore my hair like Elvis. All the b'ys teased me that I wouldn't have the nerve.

By Thursday I had the Brylcreem, and it was stowed safely away at the back of my sock and underwear drawer. I knew if my parents saw it I would be in big trouble. I'd miss my date and spend the weekend barred in the house.

After what seemed like a week of Fridays, Saturday finally came. With my chores all done, I took a bath in the big galvanized tub, brushed my teeth, and put on my good pants and shirt. The Brylcreem safely concealed inside my jacket, I set out for a night to remember. Mom allowed, as I was leaving, that there must be something up because I looked so clean and well-dressed. I was just thankful that it was not their turn to chaperone tonight.

I went down the road to John and Katie's. They were the go-to couple when you needed to keep a secret. There I socked the Brylcreem to my hair and combed it into an Elvis ducktail. It looked so good that I could almost feel that Elvis twitch in my left leg: "Thank you, thank you very much." John told me it looked like it was greased down with pork fat, but I paid him no mind.

The cold winter wind stiffened my pompadour as I walked down to meet Missy at the Split Rock, our agreed-upon meeting place. You never went to the girl's house on the first date. You'd be too scared of her parents. You would be a long way into your teens before you got that kind of nerve.

She giggled at my hair, and when I tried to kiss her on the cheek, she pushed me away. We went on down to the Orange hall. I stayed outside as she went on in ahead of me. When I opened the door to go in, I found out why. Her parents were tonight's chaperones!

Everyone turned as I opened that door, and the room went quiet as they all stared at my Elvis hair. Some of the girls giggled, and the music started. I went over to ask Missy to dance, and as I was about to do so, my best friend, Wilson, who was standing near her parents, piped up in a voice loud enough for them to hear, "I wouldn't take Missy to a dance with *my* hair like that!"

The operative word there was "take." I don't think they had any idea we were together, until Wils had to open his big mouth. The effect on her parents was like dropping gasoline on a fire. All hell broke loose. The Master of the Loyal Orange Lodge was called over and asked to "have this greasy young reprobate thrown out of the dance!"

As I was escorted toward the door, my humiliation was heightened by hearing Missy tell her giggling friends that she only asked me to "do" my hair because I dared ask her for bars and chips to ride on that "stupid horse."

In the coming days, my parents heard about the incident, and my mother was mortified. She was sure I'd come to no good. Dad was more circumspect about the whole incident, but he did go talk to the Grand Master.

"You were always against anyone who wanted to be different, as you were with my son. Don't ever make a public show of him again. If you think my son needs to be chastised, you let me know and I'll decide what is necessary—not you."

I am forever grateful that he stood up for me. I ended up forgiving Missy. What else is a little kid with a big crush on the most beautiful creature God ever allowed to be created to do?

I didn't go to church every Sunday, but I did go often, and I usually went to Sunday school. Mom wasn't going to let any horse or man interfere with her plan to educate her son, both academically and religiously. God bless her, her morals and beliefs. A great many of them have stayed with me. The night after the Brylcreem incident, she insisted I go to church. She told me to hurry to the supper table so we wouldn't be late for service. She made me say the grace.

For some reason, I remember exactly what we had. There were three kinds of potato salad (vegetable, mustard, and beet), cold meat from dinner, tea, and—as I would tell my own kids later in life—the best home-baked bread ever made. For dessert we had jelly and "lemange"—at least that's what we called it. That name had come down from Dad's mother. She never went to school a day in her life but taught herself to read and write—a remarkable woman.

For years after I left home I believed it was a special family recipe, although it always tasted much like custard to me.

One day when I was cooking for myself, I took a custard package out of the cupboard, looked at the package, and noticed that the brand name was La Manche. The same package my mother and grandmother had used to make "lemange." I laughed when I realized I had just been eating custard with a fancy name all those years.

As for church, I'd been thinking of doing an act of charity, but for that I'd need the horse. And yes, I admit it, I had an ulterior motive, too. I was going to ask Mom's permission on the way to church, but I chickened out and decided to ask her after.

I was no different than any other young boy brought up there, I suppose. We'd all been reared on the community value, as well as the religious value, of charity toward those less fortunate.

No matter how little you have, someone else has even less.

Church went well, and I couldn't believe my luck—the sermon was on charity! When church was over, the clergyman invited anyone who wanted to stay to have a singsong. This would delay my request for the horse, but at the same time, not being obstinate about staying would put me in Mom's good graces. She loved to sing.

My mother's faith was so simple and direct, I marvel when I think of it now. No scholar, no scientist—not even Darwin could ever convince her that her Creator did not exist. Her answer to that challenge was always, "So, the beauty of my flowers, the vegetables growing in my garden, the love of my family, and the order in the heavens is all an accident? Not likely." Right on, Mom.

We sang "Jesus Saviour Pilot Me," "Onward Christian Soldiers," "How Firm a Foundation," "Faith of Our Fathers," and "Just as I Am." I loved to hear her sing, and I'm not ashamed to say my eyes leaked a little sometimes when I heard her clear, vibrant voice singing praises with such absolute conviction to her God.

Soon we were out of church, walking home in the dark, and I asked Mom, "Can I do an act of charity for the widow?"

Mom couldn't believe her ears and turned her flashlight toward my face, replying, "You heard the minister, did you, my son? What do you want to do for her?"

"I'd like to take the horse, get some people, and go get her a load of wood." My mother, believing, I suppose, it was the Lord moving in mysterious ways, and that He would therefore protect her son from any accident, said, "Yes, Beaton, that would be a good thing. I'll tell your father when I get home."

I hate to disillusion you, now, but I wanted to spend the time with Missy. She had asked me if I would use my horse on Saturday to help her haul some wood for a widow who lived with her daughter and whom was not having it easy.

This being an old-fashioned winter, they were running low on wood. If I did not spend some time with Missy soon, my spirit would be broken. I would lose her, and the taunts of my schoolmates would finish me off. I would do the charity, and Missy would be a wonderful added bonus.

I remember that look of pride my dad had when Mom told him what I was about to do. Next Saturday we delivered the load of wood. I'll never forget the look on the widow's face, or her gratitude for that pile of dry stovewood. Now, years later, I wonder if I fooled either of my parents, or if I had really fooled myself. If I could go back I'd do it again, no mistake, with or without Missy.

There's no feeling quite like doing something for someone which they are unable to do for themselves. Later, as a member of the House of Assembly, I was lucky enough to get that feeling many times. Perhaps that's why I stayed at it so long.

School has to be one of the most important parts of any child's life—whether they like going or not. (I loved it.) It was there all through your childhood, and the way you remember childhood events later in life is most often by what grade you were in when they occurred.

Ours was a denominational school—United Church—and it was an old one-room building built in 1904. It has seen better days, and worse—the Depression.

My first teacher was Leah Tulk, my uncle Beaton's wife. She was strict as hell but a good teacher. There were about fifty students total, in grades one to eleven. Ten or twelve of them were about my age.

A new school was built when I was in grade four. It was still a one-roomer, but in about grade seven or eight they built a piece on. In fact, my father built it for the school board. Now there were two rooms—and two teachers! Grades one to six were in one room, and grades seven to eleven were in another.

The other teacher I remember well was Stanley Whiteway. He was from Musgrave Harbour but had moved with his family to Ladle Cove to teach. He was my teacher through grade ten in high school.

Newfoundland did not introduce grade twelve until 1979 or 1980, if memory serves. With grade eleven you could start first-year university. In Nova Scotia, and in other jurisdictions at the time, you could either start your freshman year of university after grade eleven or complete grade twelve in high school and then start second-year university upon graduating.

One of the advantages of a multi-grade classroom, at least in those days, was learning more than you were taught. What I mean is, whether you wanted to or not, you couldn't help but hear the teacher instructing the higher grades. Whether you were supposed to be doing math exercises or reading a story, you were seduced by the history or geography lessons the older kids were learning. You absorbed them and remembered them.

When you got to the next grade, it essentially became a review—at least for me. I loved to read and was driven by parents who believed that education was the key to a successful future. I had only to look at my parents, let alone those with a half-dozen youngsters, to see how tough life was for those who couldn't get a good job.

A good job in our little world was then defined as either teacher, minister, or a position working for the government. I was lucky enough to get all three!

So, by reading voraciously, studying, and by "absorption" I was lucky enough to skip grades five and eight. Then I failed grade nine! My marks were close, though, so they promoted me anyway. I passed grade ten but failed French, so I couldn't take it in grade eleven. (In those days the Protestant schools taught French. The Anglican and Roman Catholic schools taught Latin.)

I suppose it didn't matter much if you weren't going on to university, but if you were, you needed the second language, either French or Latin. In grade eleven I decided that I wanted to go on to university. I'd given it a lot of thought, as I didn't see many opportunities in Ladle Cove. I would have to go away to work anyway, so why not attend university and get a better job? One day I came home and told my parents my decision.

"Pardon my soul to God, Japh, I think we're going to make something of him!" was my mother's triumphant response.

Now I was in a quandary. I was partway through grade eleven, but if I passed—without the French—I couldn't get into Memorial University.

At the time some of the bigger five- or six-room schools—Joey's schools, we called them—were teaching French. You could get a bursary of $600 to go there. If I passed grade eleven in Ladle Cove, I couldn't get that money.

My dad, going against everything he had ever taught me, told me that I had to fail grade eleven in Ladle Cove! He had enough saved to get me through first-year university but not enough to send me to one of Joey's schools (without the bursary) for a year, and then first-year university.

I failed. I almost passed, but near the end of the year the reality of the situation struck me, and I successfully failed grade eleven. What a time I had for the rest of the school year! That fall I went off to Wesleyville to repeat grade eleven. I boarded there with a fellow named Ces Winsor.

Dad dressed up, put on his good quiff hat, and took me over to enrol. We went to see Max Mullet, the principal, and Dad did the talking. "He's bright. He could have passed in Ladle Cove, but I told him he had to fail grade eleven." Then Max said, "You what?" Dad explained. I suppose Max thought that anyone who would go to such lengths to get to university deserved a crack at it. He just smiled and nodded. I got in!

On the first day of school, Fred Best came into the class and said, "If anyone here got less than thirty-five in grade ten French, there is no use of you being here." I had gotten twenty-eight per cent. Then he walked around the room and asked everyone, individually, what their mark was. There were forty-sevens and thirty-sevens and a thirty-five, and then he came to me.

I said, "I can't tell you," and with that I got sent to the principal's

office. The principal, knowing my story, took my side and I got to stay—
and Fred was a great teacher. A good man who later became mayor of
Clarenville.

At the end of the year, the teachers all showed up at the exam room
to see how their students did.

"What do you think you got?" asked Fred.

"About eighty, I figure," I replied. I actually got eighty-three.

"Now then," he said, "what did you get in grade ten French?"

"Proved you wrong," I replied. "I got twenty-eight!"

So I graduated grade eleven with honours, but without that story I
would never have made it to university.

As far as I know, only one person from Ladle Cove went to university
before me. She would be Eleanor (Tulk) Pinsent, who played on the first
ladies' basketball team in Newfoundland. I believe the school was then
called Methodist College.

I was definitely the first from Ladle Cove with a master's degree—a
tribute more to my parents' urging that I get a good education, and to the
voice of Joey, than to me.

Sitting with my late uncle and namesake, Beaton Tulk

My father's freight boat

My dad's lumber truck

My sister, Blanche, and me with our kid goat

Left: In a sleigh being pushed across the pond by my sister, Blanche, circa 1946
Right: Cutting hay for my horse, June, circa 1961

Ladle Cove roads circa 1960

Left: Building a barn for my daughters' horse, Charlie, circa 1981
Right: Me with Bill Wellon's big fish

A stroll through "downtown" Ladle Cove

2

University and Teaching Career

OFF TO MEMORIAL

While still in grade eleven at Wesleyville I had applied for Memorial University. After some soul-searching, I decided that I wanted to be a teacher. My parents were happy about that, and I suppose the only way Mom could have been more pleased would have been if I had chosen the ministry instead.

Rev. Ray Tucker, the United Church minister during my grade eleven in Wesleyville, encouraged me to become a minister. He almost had me convinced! (My mother might have said "Almost Persuaded," like the church hymn we sang.) Another fellow tried to get me to join the RCMP.

My uncle Beaton talked me out of that. He was a WWII veteran, but he didn't think too much of someone wearing a uniform to work every day. Perhaps he thought that one Beaton Tulk in uniform, risking his life daily, as he had in the war, was enough. "Put it on and I'll take it off of you," he told me. Even then he could still have done it, too.

I was back home in Ladle Cove for the summer, of course, before I got a response to my application.

I got my hands on the letter at the post office and quickly tore it open to see what it said. What if they had too many applications and all available spots had been filled—the day before they got my application? What if my application got mislaid? My grade eleven marks were good, but there was always the chance that something could go wrong.

My parents' hopes and dreams were riding on me having a better life by getting a proper education—which they'd had no chance to do. The news was good: accepted! When I got home, let's just say that the look on their faces said it all. The look was pride—pride in that all their "preaching" and urging had paid off. And proud that they were able to get their son one step closer to a future of which his parents couldn't even dream. Yeah, it was pride—but the good kind.

At the time, if you took one year of university, you could get a grade one teaching certificate. If you didn't go to university but had your grade eleven, you could take a summer school course to learn teaching methods, and then they would issue you a grade two certificate.

Fall finally came, and I was off to St. John's. The road had been built to connect us to the rest of the world somewhere around 1959—I believe it was done when I was in Wesleyville, getting my French. Uncle Beaton drove me down to the Gambo train station, where I would board the CN train to St. John's.

The biggest place I'd ever been before was Lewisporte—on the boat with my father. St. John's was going to be an adventure. Mom reviewed the trip with me before I left and gave me a note to put in my pocket in case I forgot anything.

It read, in part, ". . . when you get off the train in St. John's, you'll see cars with a light on top. Look for one of those cars and ask them to take you to this address." I'd never even seen a taxicab before.

The train arrived in Gambo early evening, from the west. You could eat or drink on the train, but I didn't use those amenities. I had sandwiches with me—we didn't have much money, and I couldn't afford to waste it. Somewhere around 8:00 p.m. we left the station. After we got rolling, the conductor collected the tickets—the first fee I ever paid for a ride.

Having not been on a train before, I was a bit apprehensive at first, like most people would be today their first time flying. You don't want to look like an amateur, so you watch what others do. Then you do the same, acting like you'd done it a hundred times before.

The train was quite an experience. As a passenger, you can't see what is directly ahead of you. Only the engineer or someone else in the engine room can see. On a boat, on a horse, or in a plane, the driver also has the ability to manoeuvre in order to avoid obstacles.

The train, however, has a predetermined route. Everything else has to move to avoid it—a quick demise for an errant moose, or a disaster for a stalled car on a level crossing. Those engineers must have nerves of steel.

After ten or so stops and some twelve or so hours later, we arrived in St. John's. I don't think I slept at all on the train.

There was too much new stuff, here and ahead of me, to think about. What was St. John's like? How different would university be from high school?

In those days, with the denominational schools, each church had its own residence. Mine would be the United Church residence up on Long's Hill—not far from the old university building—the old one, which was just up the hill at the corner of Merrymeeting Road and Parade Street.

Our residence had three floors. The ground floor had a kitchen and dining room and administrative offices. The top floor had the male students, about twelve of us. The middle floor housed the female students—about the same number of girls as boys. We were certainly just boys and girls, no mistake—I was all of sixteen years old—and a bayman, to boot.

My roommate was a guy named Melvin Hoben. He was sent to Centreville to teach after we completed our year. He settled there, married a local woman, and stayed. Our room contained two single beds and two dressers—and nothing more that I can remember. We studied in the dining room, which doubled as study hall in the evenings.

On the first day of classes, I showed up wearing a sweater. You were supposed to wear a dress shirt, tie, and a jacket. I didn't know. The first prof in the first class pointed it out to me. It may have been covered in the information we were sent, but I probably didn't read it. The next day, I had a tie and shirt and a jacket over the top, like you would.

It was quite a disciplined way of life. We had to be in bed at a certain time and up at the appointed time. I smoked, but you couldn't do it at school or at the residence.

I really hadn't started drinking then, but one afternoon my buddy and I went out and got drunk. We were acting "silly" when we got back, and we almost got booted out. Other than that incident, I didn't get into much trouble.

Classes were between 9:00 and 6:00. Memorial University was now at its new location, on what is now University Avenue—about a twenty-minute walk from the residence. This was 1961 and the first year of the new campus. On October 9, the province held an official opening and showcased the new facility to Canada and much of the world.

Fifteen thousand or more students attended, including university students, and high school students who had been bused in from across Newfoundland, as well as representatives of almost every significant business and community organization active at the time. Prime Minister John Diefenbaker, provincial, federal, and municipal government members, and forty-one presidents of the (then) forty-two Canadian universities showed up for the big event.

US President John F. Kennedy sent Eleanor Roosevelt, the widow of former president Franklin D. Roosevelt, as his special emissary. The British sent Lord Thompson of Fleet, who became the new university's first chancellor. Choirs sang. Politicians spoke.

The Royal Jamaican Military Band played. The little guy with the bow tie and the horn-rimmed glasses was front and centre. Had he died right there, it would have taken a skilled team of undertakers to remove the smile from his face. Joey was in his glory.

Joey Smallwood did a great deal to bring the importance of education to the forefront in the minds of the province's people. He saw it as the way out of poverty—the people's means to get away from a system which victimized the worker to the degree of near-slavery. The multitude of new secondary schools and the new university were huge steps in that direction.

I thank our parents for drilling the value of education into me and others of my generation, but I am ever mindful of the source of their inspiration. It is regrettable, in my opinion, that Joey is not better remembered for all the good he accomplished as opposed to any mistakes he made. If you do nothing, you will do nothing wrong.

Soon the celebration was over and it was back to classes, studying, learning, and preparing for a teaching career. At our dorm the proctor was Rev. McKim, a United Church minister, and former chaplain, I believe, in the armed forces. The matron was Miss Barbour, a sister to Bonavista South district's former MHA Rossie Barbour. The church superintendent, however, would decide where you would teach once you completed your year at Memorial.

The United Church superintendent of education at that time was Dr. Charlie Roberts, a small, short, but authoritative man. Partway through the year he came to see me, to say where he wanted me to locate. He wanted me to go to Aspen Cove—the next community from my home in Ladle Cove, now joined by a proper road!

"Tulk," he said, looking up at me, "you're of good stock, Mr. Tulk."

"Why do you say that, sir?" I asked.

"You're a Tulk. You're a Tulk from Newtown, right? My mother was a Tulk from Newtown. Anybody that's a Tulk from Newtown has got to have good stuff in them. I need you to go to Aspen Cove. You'll do well there."

They'd had some trouble—unruly students and the like—and he thought I'd be the right person to clean it up. I wasn't crazy about the idea. I knew a lot of the young fellows from Aspen Cove—some would only be two or three years younger than me. I knew their families—their fathers and mothers. This might become a trial by fire. I thought it might be harder to keep discipline when most of them knew me. A stranger might get more respect.

I got home for Christmas break. It was nice having my own room again. I had no problem with my college roommate, but there's something to be said for having more privacy. Ladle Cove sure looked small, after St. John's. Some of my friends had gone away, a number of them off to trade school. Those who worked at the fish, or in the woods, were still around. I felt a bit like the hometown hero going home. Everyone who hadn't been far "outside" wanted to know about the big city, the sights, the sounds, the girls.

Up until Joey's time, many young guys would go to work as soon as they could, not interested in, or not able to afford to pursue, more education. Smallwood, as I've said, put a lot of effort into developing new schools and furthering education. He believed that education was the key to the future for our youth. He was right, of course. More and more parents began encouraging their children to go beyond high school, to ensure a better future.

At home now for Christmas, I had a few drinks with the boys—but not around my family. I started smoking in front of my father for the first time, though. He didn't say a word. He already knew, I suppose. It was a rite of passage in those days.

When you could smoke without hiding it from your father, you were an adult. Almost all men and a scattered woman smoked. Of course, at the time we weren't armed with all the scientific knowledge that linked smoking to lung cancer and other diseases.

I hung out with my buddies, and in the evenings we played a few games of 500s—a card game similar to bridge. (Whoever got to 500 first won the game.) This was the game of cards for grown-ups at the time. Christmas vacation went fast, and before I knew it I was back in my uncle's car, on the way to Gander this time, if I recall correctly. I believe our road had just been linked up to the Gander Bay road, which went right in to Gander. At the train station there I caught the "Newfie Bullet" again and enjoyed an even longer train ride back to school.

Nothing much exciting happened during the next term. I attended classes, studied, and, for the most part, behaved myself. We finished our coursework and wrote our exams. I believe that the end of the school year was in late April or early May.

I'd completed the year, so it was time to go home. During the summer you'd find out if you passed. The official papers and the teaching certificate, however, didn't come in the mail until September or October month. This time going home, I believe I caught a ride with another student who lived in my area. That cut the trip back to a mere six- or eight-hour run.

That summer I worked in the woods cutting pit props. They were cut like pulpwood, in four-foot lengths, and shipped from Carmanville, mostly to northern Europe for use in the mines. A local guy named Edgar Baird had the contract. I worked for him, cutting, peeling, and piling in the woods between Carmanville and Ladle Cove.

That fall, I started my career as a teacher. By now a new regional high school had been built in Carmanville, and students in grades nine to eleven went there by bus. In my school in Aspen Cove we had two rooms, one for grades one to four, and one for my class, grades five to eight. I walked the three or so miles to school a good few times. Most times, though, I hitched a ride with the high school bus, which took the higher grades to that new school in Carmanville—built while I was in university.

I was a bit nervous on the first day, as you are always nervous for a while at a new job. It comes, I suppose, from not wanting to make mistakes and being surrounded by people who have certain expectations of you. It's a little different, though, in a teaching environment. You are the leader. Your students, in effect your co-workers, know that you are better educated than them. The disrupters want to test your resolve, not your knowledge, to see if they can make a fool of you—to impress the girls, I guess.

They'd had trouble there the year before. The young guy who was teaching was asked to leave, and this opened the position for me. He just wasn't cut out to be a teacher. The school had been totally out of control. The kids ran it.

We opened school the first day of September, but we (the two teachers) were there by the middle of August. You had to air the place out, sort the textbooks and other supplies, and do up timetables. A timetable is simply a class schedule for what you would be teaching when—complicated by the fact that you had three or four grades (four the first year) in the same room. For example, you just couldn't be teaching math to two different grades at once.

On the first day of school, I had the kids draw up their own set of school rules. These were *their* rules, and making them active participants served to get them to take ownership of them. The rules were simple—be polite to others, don't disrupt class, and so on. The idea was likely something I picked up in university. I know it definitely worked.

The same day, I symbolically threw away the strap. "We all know the rules. We all agreed to them. Follow the rules or you don't get to stay here. We won't be needing this anymore," I told them. We didn't, either.

If I had a student break the rules, I made them stay after school and write lines. They would have to write the rule they broke 200 or up to 600 times, depending on the severity of the infraction. For example, "I will not disrupt class" was repeatedly written in their scribbler. Kids hate this. They want to get out after school, and if they are late getting home, in most homes they had some explaining to do.

I wanted to get home, too—but at least I could correct tests, or prepare tomorrow's lessons, while the poor little devils had to do the most boring thing on the face of God's earth. It worked, though, and soon most of the kids were strictly adhering to the rules.

I played hockey and ball with them outside. When we were outside I was one of the guys. When we were inside, however, I was Mr. Tulk and Sir. Of course, there's always a few schoolyard fights, and I had to break up the odd one.

I had a good student, Phonse Tulk, who had to write 400 or 500 lines of I-will-nots. He was supposed to be home after school to repair lobster traps. He kept saying, "My father is going to kill me. Can I do this later? My father is going to kill me!"

Finally, he wondered aloud if it was okay for him to use two pencils and do two lines at once. By firmly holding two pencils, properly spaced, between his thumb and forefinger, he was able to cut in half the time required to complete the task. I kept the lines for years. Inventive guy—and he later became very successful as a fisherman.

Some of these boys were a pretty good size. One of them, a second or third cousin, was as big as me, or bigger. I had one guy who just would not follow the new rules. Always talking back to me. And one day he called me a "god---- son of a b----." I just put him right out of school.

"You can come back," I told him, "when you are ready to apologize to the students inside. Not me—the whole class." His father showed up a little later.

He was one of the "toughs" of the community. I explained to him what I had said to his son. He was going to give me a good hiding, he told me.

"Your chance is good right now," I told him. "Close the door and we'll go outside and see who does what to whom." Out we go, and he backed away. He wasn't happy, though, so he went to see the school board member, Irving West, who was a well-respected local businessman. Irving had a general store. Anything you wanted, he had it. If not, he had it for you the next week. Buddy told Irving that I said I was going to give *him* a trimming.

"Well, so you're afraid of him? The best thing you can do, then," Irving told him, "is to take your young fellow back and get him to apologize." A couple of days later, he brought him back. He apologized to the class, and I had no further trouble with him or his father.

Another time, one of the boys was talking to a fellow student and leaning away from me instead of listening. Just to get his attention, I dropped the heavy textbook I was holding directly over his desk, expecting that the loud noise when it hit the desktop would get his attention. Somehow he was alerted to the fact that I saw him, and he turned back quickly. It hit him, or more accurately he hit the book, and it knocked him out.

I had to carry him home. His father told me, "Too bad you didn't hit him a little harder. It might've knocked some sense into him." The young fellow and I became good friends later in life. Another one of my students there was a kid by the name of Clarence Chaulk. Clarence went on to become very successful in contracting and retail—and a good friend. I even went into business with him for a time.

Another event I remember was a yearly concert we'd give at the school just before Christmas. We'd do some Christmas songs and recitations and a lot of other stuff, too. For example, a play—not just Christmas-related. I suppose there were a few kids trying to disrupt or make the ones on stage forget their lines—like I had at the church Easter concert a few years earlier. They were mostly well-behaved, though.

The two-room school was divided by a wall, but there were four or five doors you could take down and open the whole space up into one room, with a stage put up at one end. We'd get chairs from community organizations, and the majority of the community would come together for the event. There were a total of about fifty-five students there at the time.

The school had a wood and coal stove. The coal was something new. Previously all students had to bring a junk of wood to school each day. It was the same in Ladle Cove when I went to school. By the time winter came, they had a good stockpile. Now, the coal stove cut down on a lot of that.

We had two different teachers while I was there for the other class—Wilena Wellon, and then Marie Pennell. I believe Wilena had her grade eleven and summer school, and she made $106 a month. Marie had the same as me, one year university, and she made about $200 a month. I was hauling down a grand total of $240 a month!

Before you bring up gender equality, I'll tell you why I was making more. I was the principal of the whole school—all two rooms of it! I got the principal's bonus for that.

Marie and Wilena were both very good teachers, no mistake, and it was enjoyable working with them. Strange that, when I was fourteen, I wasn't sure I'd make it to university because of French. The deficiency was corrected, of course, and I was a school principal at the grand old age of seventeen!

In summer, when school was out, I went back in the woods cutting burnt wood. There had been a big fire, one of the biggest we ever had, the Bonavista North fire that burned from Gambo down through to Ladle Cove.

We were salvaging what was usable for pulpwood. It was first thrown in a pond, soaked, and then put through a debarking machine. At the end of the day, you'd be black from head to toe. Dirty, hard work, and I loved it.

I continued to live in Ladle Cove while I was teaching in Aspen Cove, first at my parents' house, and later in another house when I got married at age twenty in 1964. I married a girl named Barbara, from my home community, who is the mother of my three children.

One of the few true tragedies of my life happened during those years. My uncle Beaton took sick. He was having heart problems, but he told nobody in the family about it. He bought a schooner and went down on the Labrador to fish. In spite of the fact that he was one of the best seamen around, he put his vessel up on the rocks and decided to come home. Probably had a weak spell.

He and my father were piling nets up on the twine loft. He didn't feel well, so he climbed down. It was too hot for him. Dad found him leaning over the back of his car.

He died there, suddenly, at the side of the bank. Uncle Beaton was only forty-four years old when he passed away in 1964. I was twenty-two. He was a well-respected guy—a war veteran, an able sailor, and a good man—and he went way too young.

Later, I bought his car from his widow, my aunt Leah. I believe it was for a token price of $500 or something like that. The same car Uncle Beaton had used to drive me down to the Gambo train station when I went to Memorial, my first year. It was a 1960 Chevy Biscayne.

In my fourth year at Aspen Cove, I started getting restless for something different in the teaching area, and I got transferred to the bigger six-room elementary school in Carmanville. I taught grade four that year. It was different, but I still wanted more. I loved teaching, no mistake. The only thing I loved better than teaching was learning.

I starting thinking about going back to university to learn more and to get a higher teaching certificate, as the approach to education was changing. I knew I would need more to continue progressing in this profession. With one year of university I had a grade one, and with a degree I could get a grade four. With two degrees I could get a grade five, and with a master's, a grade seven.

As I looked around, more and more people were getting higher education. Traditionally, education was rated low by the poor. Until Joey

Smallwood, little emphasis was put on it. No child was compelled to go to school until age seven.

Earlier, before Joey, many never even went *at all*. Education was something that belonged to the well-to-do. It wasn't seen as a way to a better life, a way out of poverty.

I intended to stay teaching at the time, so it made sense to do it, now or never. With that, I went back to Memorial from 1967 to 1970 and completed coursework to graduate in 1970 with two degrees—B.A. and B.Ed. We moved to town during those years, and my wife worked, I worked during the summers, and I accessed some student loans to get through.

That first summer, I worked as a labourer on the community stage in Ladle Cove. The next summer, I worked out at the cement plant in White Hills, making cement culverts for the Department of Transportation.

The following summer, I decided that I wanted to make more money. I could have gone back to the cement plant, but I wanted to make as much as I could during the summer.

I put an application in for Churchill Falls, which was then being built, but there were hundreds of people applying. At the time, Roy Legge was the CEO, and he later became a cabinet minister with Joey Smallwood.

I figured I'd better try to fast-track my application if I was to have any hope of a job. So, I went down to Confederation Building to see Joey. I made it up to the eighth floor, but I was stopped there by the receptionist, an older man.

"What can I do for you, sir?"

"I want a job, and I came here to speak with the premier."

"Well . . . the premier is very busy, you know."

"I'll wait. He has to come out of his office sometime today. I see his car is down there"—the big old Chrysler Imperial he used to drive—"so if I can't see him here, I'll see him down there."

"Well, what are you looking for?"

"I want to go to Churchill Falls to work."

"Well, then," he said, "you don't have to see the premier for that.

There's a guy in an office over there who can handle that matter for you. I'll take you in to see him."

So he did, and I was introduced to a guy by the name of C. Maxwell "Max" Button, who had earlier been the MHA for Trinity South.

"Where are you from, by the way?" Max asked me.

"Ladle Cove."

"Good. I know Ladle Cove fairly well. What are you looking for?"

"I'm looking for a job at Churchill Falls."

"Any particular kind of job?"

"No, I don't care what it is. I just want to work. I can drive a truck—I learned to drive in a five-ton truck—but any kind of work would be good."

With that, Max picked up the phone and called Roy Legge, CEO of the Churchill Falls (Labrador) Corporation, and said, "I've got a young fellow with me here. The premier is a very good friend of the family, and he'd like him to get a job at Churchill Falls." Yeah, that's what he did!

Within two days I had my stuff all packed in my old "chariot" and was on my way to Churchill Falls. I broke down near Clarenville—the water pump was gone—and I got it towed into Decker's in Clarenville to be fixed. Then I was off again. I made it back to Ladle Cove, unloaded, packed some clothes for the summer, and then drove back to Gander. I flew from there to Churchill Falls. My first time on an airplane!

Lloyd Jones, of the manpower division for Churchill Falls, met me up there at the airport, and we filled out some papers before I got started. Another guy, Lemuel Pickett, who was new, too, was teamed up with me, and we worked together on a variety of odd jobs—cutting down trees, setting in poles, running wires, and scaling big rocks off the cliffs above the intakes. We were seventy-five feet up in the air, beating loose rocks off the walls to prevent injury to people and vehicles working below.

The old skipper, Pete Posey, got to like us, and he wanted us to go to work underground. It was better money, and that's what I was after. So that's what we did. From working seventy-five feet up in the air on an eight-inch plank to installing rock bolts underground—that's how I spent the summer of 1969.

I came back with $5,700 out of it and went right out and bought myself a new car. The old Biscayne had over 300,000 miles on it from Uncle Beaton's time and all my driving back and forth to university. I was due for a new one.

I bought a new Ford Custom from George G. R. Parsons, the then Ford dealer on Elizabeth Avenue.

I got that summer job through Joey Smallwood, although I didn't get to see him in the spring of 1969. I had met him before, though, when I was in grade nine. Goodyear and Sons were completing the final 500-foot section of the road that links Ladle Cove to Aspen Cove and to the main road. Up on the hill there, where the ribbon was cut and Joey spoke, the area became known as Joey's Hill. I met Joey down at the church after the ceremony.

The Goodyears, who originated from Ladle Cove, had put up prizes for the best essays from students in grades nine to eleven about the importance of roads to the development of Newfoundland. The presentations were done at the church. I won the first prize, $50, and Joey presented the prizes.

But back to 1969. I finished my final year at Memorial and graduated in the spring of 1970 with my B.A.

In the spring of 1970, we moved back to Ladle Cove, and that fall I commuted daily to Carmanville, where I taught grade nine with my new grade five teaching certificate.

I always enjoyed teaching math, but later I got more interested in English—or h'English, as my crowd calls it. (That's just the way we talk, sure.) The important thing is: do you communicate? I recall, back in university, one course which all students were sent to: speech class. It wasn't a credit course, but they wanted to "correct" our English.

As anyone knows, if they've heard me speak, I drop the "H" and h'add it on where it doesn't belong. This is essentially the Dorset, or West Coast England, way of speaking. These people—my ancestors—left there and came directly to isolated outports in Newfoundland. With very little outside contact, the dialect remains almost pure to this day.

I remember on the first day of this class at Memorial, the professor gave us each two words to pronounce. Mine were "hearth" and "cloister." I'm pretty sure you know what happened with that first one.

"That's not good English," the prof said.

"What is good English?" I asked her. "Is it the way they speak on CBC, the way they speak in the southern USA, or the way the Queen speaks?" I explained that we all have regional dialects, and as long as one is understood, that's all that matters. As long as you are making yourself understood, you are communicating effectively. I told her that I would not give up my historical English for the one she taught.

"I think you're being a bit uppity," she told me. "If you refuse to pronounce it right, then there's no room in this class for that."

"Apparently not," I said, and then I walked "h'out." Didn't go back, either. She was a Newfoundland woman, too. She should have known better.

I stayed teaching in Carmanville for three years. On July 30, 1971, my first child, Cynthia, was born.

In the winter of 1972, I received an invitation from Dr. Philip Warren of Memorial University to return for my master's. I decided to do so in order to get as far as I could in my field and then try to apply what I learned to education here in my little corner of the world. In 1973, I went back to Memorial University for my master's. Things went smoothly. As part of my work, I was assigned to go to Ontario to do a study of community schools in Leeds-Grenville. I stayed in Brockville under the tutelage of the great educator Lloyd Dennis.

For three and a half months I was privileged to work with this amazing guy, co-author of the groundbreaking Hull-Dennis report to the Ontario Royal Commission on Education in 1968: "Living and Learning." I learned about how an education system should be run, how it should be administrated, about educating adults in the community, and how to use the schools as a community tool.

Lloyd grew up in a remote community in Muskoka, Ontario. Like me, he was the son of hard-working parents, in northern Ontario's lumberwoods industry. He became a major guru in the field of education and was awarded membership in the Order of Ontario and the Order of

Canada. A former teacher, principal, consultant, and education director, he had enough letters behind his name to do a second alphabet. His ideas were revolutionary, and many of his recommendations were implemented in Ontario and elsewhere.

Meeting him was a watershed time in my life. He was relaxed and so in tune with common people. His attitude toward his staff was as if they were family. I remember one time that we walked into his office—about thirty-five people working there, I suppose—and one of the junior staffers said, "Dr. Dennis, you need a haircut." He simply turned around, went out, got his hair cut, and then came back. Another time we were at a big dinner—a seven-course meal—and when his turn to speak came, he got up and said, "Great meal, but not as good as my mother used to cook, back in the lumbercamp."

Along with being a teacher and mentor to me, he became a good friend. Later, he and his wife, Cathy, came down to Ladle Cove to visit me. They stayed with us a couple of days, loved the area, and enjoyed talking with the local folks. He fit right in—after all, he had come from a similar background. He left me a really good bottle of wine. I kept the bottle of wine for about twenty years.

I went to visit him, too—the last time was in 2011. He had retired in Orillia, back to the area from whence he came. He passed away the next year, 2012, at the age of eighty-eight. When I got the bad news, I sat down and drank that bottle of wine.

As the *Toronto Star* said in its headline upon his death, "Lloyd Dennis redefined learning in Ontario." He was that influential on my thinking as well. Of all the people who have had a strong influence on my life, Lloyd was right at the top.

There's little else I can remember about my last time at Memorial, certainly nothing that comes close to the magnitude of Lloyd Dennis's effect on my thinking.

In 1975, I went back to Carmanville with a grade seven teaching certificate and became the coordinating principal of the Carmanville school system. Six elementary schools (primary to grade seven) were then located at Davidsville, Carmanville, Frederickton, Noggin Cove, Ladle

Cove, and Aspen Cove, and we had the regional high school (grades eight to eleven) in Carmanville.

Davidsville had been shut down, but I convinced the school board to reopen it. We brought in portable school rooms, and it opened again. I was principal of the Carmanville elementary school and coordinating principal of all the other schools in the area.

I also got quite involved with student extracurricular activities, particularly sports. I coached volleyball for a while. I was a regular at taking the teams to tournaments. The coaches and parents all pitched in to take our teams and cheerleaders across the island to individual games and tournaments with other schools.

We were in the "B" Division, based on the size of the community. The "A" Division included the bigger schools from St. John's, Gander, and Grand Falls. I remember one trip when we were going to a basketball tournament in Corner Brook, or somewhere on the west coast, when I had some car trouble. My old brown 1970 Ford Custom lost its power and started making a clicking noise around Bishop's Falls.

I made it to Grand Falls, where Dave Gilbert—who later became a personal friend, a political supporter, as well as a successful politician in his own right—owned Beothuk Ford. They put the car on "the scope," which was something relatively new at the time, to determine the problem. To make a long story short, it needed a motor job or a new motor.

The choices were a) rent a car, or b) buy a new one. If I rented a car, we would have to stop on the way back to change cars again—if mine was even ready. If not, that would complicate the trip even more.

It had been almost an hour since we stopped, and the players were still in my car. None of us wanted to be late for the first game.

They say that there is more than one way to skin a cat, but once the cat is skinned you can't go back and re-skin him. I decided that I'd better do things right the first time.

I made a quick dash into the showroom and saw a demonstrator model Ford Custom on display. An employee had been driving it for a while, but it looked as good as new. The salesman came out, and I asked him how much he wanted for the car.

He gave me the price, and I told him, "If you'll take my car in trade and $3,900, I'll take it off your hands." His boss agreed to the deal.

We made a quick job of switching passengers and equipment to the new car and were gone in minutes. This car had lots of power, so I made up for lost time from Grand Falls to Corner Brook. Our game was only delayed by fifteen or twenty minutes.

The salesman later told me that he wished all sales had been that easy. "It's the first time," he said, "that I didn't have to *sell* the car—the customer sold it to himself."

We didn't have a great gym in Carmanville. It was little more than a recreation room. We went to St. Lawrence one year for the provincial championships, and they had one of the new, bigger schools. At the time, Don Jamieson was our federal minister, and under the Department of Regional Economic Expansion (DREE), he was having these bigger "DREE" schools built. I remember mentioning to our boys' basketball coach, Dennis Ryan, that our whole school would fit into the gym of this new one.

Our team was used to a much smaller court and fourteen-foot ceilings, but we did well—losing the series by only one game! We lost to the team from Belanger High in Codroy Valley. We had a couple of guys who had just moved back from Lab City and had played in the bigger facilities—they were a great help and passed their skills on to the other guys on our team.

I fought with my boss, Hudson Davis, school superintendent of the Gander Region, to get a new elementary school in Carmanville. Hudson was a good man, and we got along well, and yes, I knew there was only so much money to go around. We badly needed a new school, though. I felt that I had to fight for it.

I told him that if there was not an agreement for a new school in Carmanville by September, I would close the school. I would be on the picket line. He would then have to fire me for insubordination.

He looked at me and said, "You'd do it, too, wouldn't you?"

"Yes," I told him.

Hudson worked on it, found the money somewhere, and we got it done. We got three more, too: a new four-room school—Sandstone

Elementary—for Ladle Cove, one for Frederickton, and we brought back Davidsville.

I didn't do all this alone, of course. I got a lot of support from the communities and others, including the media. I was able to get the news media out there to show them the need, and that sure helped.

Like anything else, if something bad happens on your watch, you have to accept responsibility for it. But if something good happens which you fought hard for, perhaps you can take a little credit. I was now thirty or thirty-one, I believe. I stayed as principal there in Carmanville for five years.

Other than births and deaths, most things in life arrive or change slowly. A welder, for example, doesn't decide overnight to be a carpenter. Maybe he admires the work of the carpenter and, over time, does a bit of it himself, finds it rewarding, and becomes drawn into a different orbit.

So it was with me and politics. As a teacher, particularly in those smaller communities, you are looked up to. You are respected and sought after for advice. Perhaps someone wanted to apply for a job in another community. When they asked, you provided the best reference you could in order to help them out. If an adult needed an important form filled out, or a letter written, you helped them with it.

Soon people in the community were coming to you for help in getting things for the community—to get a new school, or get the road graded.

Maybe your students needed summer jobs so they could save money for university. You went after the MHA for any programs that might be available. If the fishing season was poor, you tried to find out about any make-work projects that could bridge the gap.

Because you were considered a concerned and responsible person, often you were then asked to apply to supervise such projects. You did it to ensure that the work was shared fairly and that the result was acceptable under the program.

If by reason of skill or luck you are able to get things done, the next thing you know, the community is coming to you for more and more help.

I got involved with everything and everyone. Every committee or organization which I was asked to join or assist, I did. I used to joke that the only reason I did not join the Ladies' Auxiliary is that they couldn't find a skirt big enough for me—and of course you could not wear pants to the meetings.

When you are able to deliver for your own people something they might not have gotten otherwise, it is a wonderful feeling. It becomes addictive. But before I get into my time in politics, I'd like to get into my business involvement, since it overlaps with the political years, even if its duration was quite short.

Teaching in Aspen Cove, 1962–63

Left: With my dog, King, and my nephew Wayne in 1972
Right: Getting my scholarship from Joey Smallwood

The house in which I grew up

My Aspen Cove students

Sunday afternoon in Ladle Cove, 1964

3

Business Ventures

MR. HARDWARE

I was elected as MHA for the Fogo district in 1979 and began my political career. First, though, I'd like to discuss my foray into the business world.

During the period of my first two terms in politics, I had a trailer set up in Pippy Park in St. John's for the summers. It was sort of a home away from home and a place to relax in the evenings. Even when the House of Assembly wasn't sitting, I still had work to do in my office at Confederation Building—when I wasn't back in my constituency in Fogo district. My family came there during the summer, and it was a great spot for the youngsters.

A very good friend of mine, and a former student at Ladle Cove, Clarence Chaulk, had a trailer set up nearby. (Clarence also helped with my election campaigns.) One day early into my second term, in 1982, we got talking and he said that he was thinking about building a strip mall on the back of Carmanville. It was Crown land, and I told him that I would try to get the land for him.

One night we met in Gander. It was about the land, I believe, and we went for a drive. We were out on McCurdy Drive, just where you come into Gander there from the Gander Bay road. We passed by an empty store on the corner of Carr Crescent. It had housed a masonry business before, built and owned by Gerald Winsor. It was closed down now, as he had gotten out of the business.

"There's the perfect place for your store," I told Clarence. "Perfect for a business."

"Think so, Cocky?" he asked. That's what he always called me, Cocky or Cock, as in cock of the walk.

"Yeah, perfect spot," I told him.

Anyway, we didn't know who owned it at the time. We found out, went to see him, and had a look at the property. We negotiated a price and secured the building. Somewhere along the way, Clarence had decided that it should be a building supply and hardware store. Clarence was already in construction, mostly working with earth-moving equipment. He did this work under his first company, Aspen Cove Enterprises.

He wanted to get into building supplies, though. I guess he was probably thinking of getting into more actual construction, of houses and other buildings. Come to think of it, I believe he had already started building some houses for Newfoundland and Labrador Housing. With the store he could do what they call a vertical integration of the two businesses. He could supply himself, so to speak. Knowing Clarence, I'm sure that he was bright enough and far-sighted enough to visualize it.

There were two other similar stores there at the time: ABM and the Home Hardware. Clarence had never even worked in a store and knew very little about retail. We didn't have enough sense to know there might not be room enough for three similar stores in the same market!

The next thing he wanted me to do was write a business plan for the store, so I did. His next move was to form a company and seek financing. We set up the company as Northeast Ltd.—a nod to our geographical location. After I finished the plan, he said to me, "I don't have enough money to do this alone. I want you to come into the business with me."

These were the days of twenty-two per cent interest rates, an economy in recession, and the banks very hesitant to take any risk. Clarence already had a guy named Oliver Coles who had worked with him and was willing to invest as a partner. I had a few dollars saved by that time, so I went in, too. I knew Clarence's work ethic. I knew his determination. If he couldn't make the business work, it sure wasn't going to be by neglect. I trusted him.

Clarence had been successful in everything he put his hand to. He was a hard worker—by that I mean up every day at 6:00 a.m. and working until 11:00 p.m. Clarence was a guy who could make you believe in him. He dropped out of school in grade eight or nine, I believe—not because he was lazy, but because he was restless. He wanted to get working.

We capitalized the company with $100,000 equity—a third each from Oliver, Clarence, and me. I wasn't involved with the day-to-day operation of the business and didn't work in the store. I talked with Clarence once a month about how the business was doing, and that was just about my only involvement.

Because Clarence was involved in other projects, we needed a manager, so we hired a guy who stayed for a short time. Then Grant Chaulk took the reins.

Grant, a cousin of Clarence, started on November 6, 1982—first day of the renovations—and stayed until the store finally closed thirty years later, then under new ownership. Good manager equals good results.

Clarence joined the Castle buying group right away and proceeded to renovate the building. Castle was not a supplier or distributor of product, per se, but simply an umbrella organization through which Clarence purchased product. The suppliers shipped to us, invoiced Castle, and Castle sent us a monthly statement. We paid Castle, and Castle then paid the suppliers, and they collected supplier rebates for us.

So, Laurie Blackwood Pike, who was the retail services manager at the hardware distributor, Sumner's, had a store plan drawn up, recommended what we should stock, and sent a crew over from Moncton to set up the store fixtures and merchandise the product.

He sold the b'ys on the Mr. Hardware franchise program—Sumner's first such store in Newfoundland—and we branded the store as Mr. Hardware Home Centre. Sumner had some private-label products, a wide assortment of hardware, and flyers we could use.

A member of the set-up crew was John Power, who merchandised the paint department with Sico Paint and who knew the line well. He met some people in Gander and liked the area so much that he quit his job at Sumner and went to work for us. He looked after the paint.

One of the things we brought in and put on display was a custom-made, fire-engine red, heart-shaped whirlpool bathtub similar to a Jacuzzi. It was an eye-catcher, for sure. It attracted a lot of attention, as you wouldn't see something like this even in St. John's at the time. We sold it, too. I remember an excited Clarence saying to me after he put it up on display, "Come here, Cocky, till I shows you what I got!"

The store opened for business late March 1983. I attended the grand opening and popped into the store sometimes when I was in Gander. We were lucky—it turns out that you make your own niche in a market, even if that segment is saturated, by doing things differently. Clarence's motto had a lot to do with it, I'm sure: "Service is everything."

As the business grew, Oliver decided he wanted to get his money out and do other things with it. So, about three years in, Clarence and I bought his share, and now we had $50,000 each and a fifty-fifty partnership in the business. They say that such a relationship is a recipe for disaster. Perhaps it would have been if I were there second-guessing Clarence's every move. But as a silent partner, I stayed away.

As a businessman, Clarence knew what he had to do to make it work, and he did. One year he shipped over seventy house lots of materials to Labrador. At its peak, Mr. Hardware did over $7 million in annual sales.

It started off slow, however, and the business struggled to meet its commitments. Clarence believed in keeping to his suppliers' payment terms, and he was proud to be able to do so. After we got the store open, he decided that we needed more time to pay for the opening order of hardware.

We had gotten thirty or forty-five days payment terms from Laurie, but as I said earlier, it took a little while for the business to gain traction. Laurie thought he could talk to his boss and get the payments spread out a bit, but he felt we could get the best deal if we flew to Moncton and had a heart-to-heart with his boss. Clarence was flat out with other projects, but I was able to go. Laurie met me at the Moncton Airport, and we drove over to see his boss at Sumner's on St. George Boulevard.

Edwin Allison "Ed" Hosford took us into his corner office. Ed was VP and general manager of Sumner. He didn't own the company, but he certainly ran it. Ed was a big guy—and probably age sixty or so then—a country boy from up on the Miramichi. He'd fought in World War II and then came home and got involved in the hardware industry.

"I like you lads," he told me, and inquired about Clarence. "I think you'll do well. According to Laurie and the pictures I've seen, you have a good operation there. Now, let's get the important business out of the way first. Let's go to lunch!"

The three of us got into Ed's big white Chrysler New Yorker and drove up to Vito's (Italian and Greek) restaurant on Mountain Road. We got seated and placed our orders. Then Ed turned to me and said, "Laurie tells me you need a little help on the opening order. What do you need, Beaton?"

"Well, Ed," I told him, "if you could see your way clear to spread the payment over three months—a third each month—it would be very helpful."

"Consider it done, Beaton. Now let's eat!"

Clarence was able to make the payments on time, and we were off to the races, so to speak. The first year we did only $800,000 in sales but had a net profit of $1,700.

We ran into another little snag later, and once again Hosford came to our rescue. By now Laurie had left Sumner Co. and had bought a building supply yard just down the Petitcodiac River from Moncton and renamed it Grandpa Pike's.

Our building had only a small back room. We had lots of room in the yard for lumber but very limited space inside to keep drywall and other products that needed to be kept under cover. At the time we had only a small operating line of credit from the bank. We needed a warehouse.

Taking that money out of our line of credit would cripple us in paying our current accounts. We went to the bank to get a long-term loan, and the bank manager told us, "Build it out of inventory and your line of credit, and when it's done we'll move into a long-term loan."

We constructed the building on good faith and then went back to the bank. The manager told us, "I just can't see my way clear to do that right now." Who knows what his problem was? Maybe he'd recently had a big loan go bad or something. Crippled by this cash flow problem, we were barely meeting our commitments and were getting quite behind on our payments to Sumner through the Castle Group.

The bank, however, had put us in a real bind. Sumner owned our inventory—they were a secured creditor.

So we called Hosford. We had a great relationship with him. He thought I was okay, but he was really fond of Clarence. A few months earlier, Clarence had put a bucket of ice over his head at his birthday party—which we had been invited to—and Hosford thought it was funny as hell.

Hosford came down to see us. We showed him the new warehouse and explained to him again what had happened.

"Oh, I see," said Hosford. "Then let's go and see this *gentleman*. Clarence, would you give Beaton the keys to the store?"

I didn't know why he wanted me to have them, but we both trusted him. Clarence gave me the keys. Hosford called the bank manager and told him he was coming in to see him about the Mr. Hardware account. The banker made time to see us, and we went on up.

Sitting there in the banker's office, Hosford spoke first.

"You know, these two boys I have here with me, I like them, and they owe me quite a bit of money. I understand that you promised them that if they put their operating line into a new warehouse, you would take care of it, move it over to a capital cost, and they would have it back in their account. Is that right?"

"Yes," said the banker, "that's right, but we can't see our way clear now to do it."

"Well, sir," said Hosford, "it goes like this." Then, turning to me, he said, "Beaton, give me the keys." I handed him the keys, wondering what would happen next. "Now," he said, "I've got the keys in my hand. By four o'clock tomorrow morning, that store is going to be empty of inventory. I've done it before, and I'll do it again.

"Now, I know," he went on, "we only have second place behind the bank, but that doesn't matter. By four a.m. the inventory will be gone, the store will be empty . . . unless . . . by three o'clock this afternoon you can change your mind on this and put that capital cost back into their line of credit. We're going up to the Albatross now—Beaton, Clarence, and I— and we *may* have a drink, and I expect to hear from you by three o'clock."

We walked out of the bank, and on the way to the car, Hosford said, "This is done now. This is done. Let's go up and have a drink." We went to the Albatross, and five minutes to three, the phone rang.

"Okay," said the banker.

That's an example of how Hosford stood behind his dealers. Six months later we cleared our account at that bank and went with the CIBC, whose manager was very helpful and treated us right.

I got out of the business in 1989. I was defeated in the election that year and accepted a civil service job. I became assistant deputy minister of Child Welfare and Youth Corrections. After I got the job, I found out that I might be in a conflict of interest because I had part ownership in this business.

I should have put it in a trust, like a lot of others did—and made some more money on it—but I sold out instead, to Clarence. So, in six or seven years, I got back five times what I had put in, as the business was much more valuable now.

Later, Clarence bought a company in Gander which sold recreational vehicles like snowmobiles and four-wheelers, and then another in the same business in Happy Valley–Goose Bay. Eventually he got the contract for the water and sewer lines in Natuashish—the resettled community of Davis Inlet, which they moved from an island onto the mainland of Labrador. Clarence was successful with everything he touched.

Now with a lot of employees in his various companies, Clarence asked me to emcee his Christmas party. I remember praising him, to his staff, as one of the best, and by the audience's response it was clear the employees felt the same way. Clarence and I had a drink together after the party wrapped up, and he thanked me. I posed a question to him.

"Clar, how successful would you have been if you had gotten an education?"

"Cocky, I probably would have been as silly as you," he responded quickly, as he always did, with a sense of humour and with no regrets.

He loved flying, and I think he caught the bug when he was young and working with a company stringing wires on transmission lines. Clarence was the one who stepped out on the helicopter's ski to drop the bolts in. He was fearless.

Clarence wanted me to take a flying course with him, but I declined. He went at it alone, spending countless hours studying manuals and doing flights. He passed all his tests with flying colours, and when he got his pilot's licence, he bought himself what he called a souped-up Cessna 185. He bought the plane from the Newburg family in Ontario.

The son, Jason Newburg, knew all the tricks—rolls, flying upside down, you name it—and taught them to Clarence. Jason is down in the US now and a top-rate aerobatic pilot. Clarence and Jason became good friends, and Jason flew down to Aspen Cove several times to visit him.

As a matter of fact, Jason and his fiancée, Clarence and his wife, Marilyn, along with my wife, Dora, and I, spent a week together island-hopping in the Bahamas in Clarence's Navajo. It was the most enjoyable vacation I ever had. Clarence's joy and love of life was intoxicating. Whatever he was going to do, you knew it would be an adventure, and you never hesitated to jump aboard.

Another time when I was in St. John's, as an MHA, Clarence called me there on a Saturday. He was in St. Joseph's constructing a senior citizens' home. He asked me if I would bring out his pickup—which he had left in town—the next morning, Sunday. Happy to help, I said sure I would. Then he gave me a list of building materials he wanted picked up and put on the back of her! The next morning, I arrived in St. Joseph's, where Clarence and his crew were in a rented trailer.

"Cocky," he said to me, "you can cook. How about cooking Sunday dinner for the boys?" So I did. After we ate, he said, "That was a good feed. Now you and me should put in some sewage disposal pipes."

What could I say? We got started, and the weather turned to sleet, and then snow. After grumbling that he didn't know if he could find a suit of rubber clothes to fit my rather large and bulky frame, he got me suited up and we spent the rest of the day shovelling crushed stone down into a ditch. I was pretty well worn out when we finished, but we got it done. Clarence turned to thank me for my help and said, "Thanks, Cocky. Now I can say I am the only guy to ever get a politician down working in a ditch."

Since he was doing a number of projects in Labrador, Clarence next bought two Aztecs—work planes that could carry heavy loads—for use up there. And finally he bought a Navajo, a two-engine, eight-seat executive plane. I flew with him many times. He was a very skilled pilot.

He'd built a Quonset hut for the Cessna, and then when he got the Aztecs, he built a big hangar to house all his planes. He had already constructed a runway out on the marsh by his home. I remember it was the middle of the winter and there he was, out working with an excavator. He dug two wide parallel trenches in the marsh, throwing all of the fill into the centre. When it had dried out and compacted down, he added more fill and gravel and then paved 1,500 feet of it. I believe at the time he had the only privately owned paved airstrip in Newfoundland. He had quite a compound there, and we all took to calling it Southfork, after the ranch in the TV series *Dallas*.

He had the strip lighted as well. He'd let Marilyn, his wife, know when he would be home, and she'd turn on the lights. He had another plane at the time, too, and he was in the process of selling it. He and I were up flying in it one evening. I had to leave to go do something, and Clarence had a young fellow coming later who was interested in buying it. They went up in it, and the engine stalled. Clarence told him not to worry: "I've got this plane."

He took it into a dive, and buddy thought he was going to crash it into the treetops to break the fall. But he was just trying to get the speed up. It worked. He pulled it up and swooped over the woods and put her down safely in the nearby bog. The next day, Clarence was up there in some sort of a tracked vehicle and towed her out from the bog to the road. Then he loaded her up on a flatbed, sideways—way too wide a load—and slowly drove her back to his place.

One winter day he, Oliver Coles, Clarence's son-in-law, and I were going to Fogo Island from his cabin at Raft Pond. The Cessna was amphibious—he had skis on it. It had sleeted and frozen the night before, and everything was covered in glitter. We heated antifreeze on the stove and poured it over the wings to de-ice them. Then we took off for Fogo.

As soon as we got up into the air, I sensed by watching Clarence that something was wrong. I asked him, "What's up? What's up?" "She won't show me the airspeed," he told me. Neither one of us knew anything about it at that point. Just north of Raft Pond is Gull Pond, and Clarence put her down there. Without knowing the airspeed, he had to guess, and she bounced—pretty hard. (Oliver wanted to get out and walk home.)

Clarence figured out that the beeping sound we had been hearing meant she was getting ready to stall because the airspeed was too slow. We came up off the pond again, and I asked, "You've got it fixed?"

"No, but I know how to do this now," he told me.

To be on the safe side, Clarence had decided to go back and land at Raft Pond. Soon we were on approach, with Oliver and me in the back seat. As we slowed, the beeping began again, of course. At the far end of the pond was a snowmobile. Oliver hollered out to Clarence, "Clar! Clar! Never mind blowing your horn at the f---er on the skidoo, just pitch this thing down!" We all got into a laughing fit, and Clarence had to go back up and bring her around again.

"Shut up this time," Clarence said to Oliver. "That beep was just the sound of her stalling and that I have to give her a little more power to land." Oliver went white, but he said no more. When we landed, Clarence figured it out. We looked her all over, and the pitot tube was frozen over— that's the tube that the wind comes in through so the gauge measures your airspeed. So we thawed it out, and that solved the problem.

Clarence had the Navajo on his final flight. He shouldn't have, as it wasn't a work plane. His plan was to load in Gander and take off there, where they had a long runway. He was supposed to land in Goose Bay, where they also have long runways. At the last minute—about nine thirty at night—a young fellow from Musgrave Harbour called him and asked if he would drop him off in Charlottetown, Labrador.

Clarence knew him. Buddy was going up there to work. So, to help out, of course he agreed to take him. He shouldn't have. Charlottetown has a short runway. He got down okay and dropped the guy off, but he couldn't get up again.

At the end of the runway you have to go up over a group of trees. He couldn't get up over them, so he decided to try to land on the highway, which was then under construction. He kept the landing gear up to maintain his airspeed.

I spoke to a Mountie up there after, and he told me that only for a load of gravel he'd have gotten down okay. They had just dumped a big load of gravel there for use in putting up a signpost. His wing clipped the pile, and it sheared off into the rock face. There was no way he could hold it. He died almost instantly.

I was in St. John's at the time this happened. About two weeks later, I was in St. Anthony and spoke to a pilot from Air Labrador by the name of Powell. I didn't know him, but I knew his father from Charlottetown quite well. He knew me and called me over.

"You lost your buddy," he told me.

"Yeah," I said.

"I've got to tell you something," he said. "That day in Charlottetown, with the downdraft and the crosswind, there was no way that plane was coming out of there. If he had his Aztec he would have come out of it all right, but not that plane. She wasn't coming out."

It was with a heavy heart that I went back to Aspen Cove to bury my best friend. I gave his eulogy at the funeral service. If was the biggest funeral I'd ever seen for someone who wasn't a celebrity, a head of state, or something like that. We didn't hold it in the church in Aspen Cove because it had a capacity of only eighty or a hundred people. Marilyn, Clarence's wife, and his daughters Trina and Tanya agreed that the hangar was the appropriate place to have the ceremony.

We had Clarence's hangar cleared out, and we put together a platform and an altar for the clergy at one end. Then we set up 400 chairs. When the time came, we had to open the big hangar doors to accommodate the several hundred more who couldn't get in. They arrived by plane and helicopter and car, and of course all the local people came. There were at least 700 there, in this small, remote area: prominent business people, friends, and neighbours. I was there along with former premier Brian Tobin, and then current premier Roger Grimes.

When it came time to do the eulogy, I can truly say that it was the toughest job I ever had to do in my public life. At the same time, though, I could almost hear Clarence whisper, "Some crowd, eh, Cocky?"

Everyone who met Clarence Chaulk or did business with him liked him. I remember years later, when I was living in the Goulds, having a heat shield made to go behind my wood stove in the shed. I went to a sheet metal shop to have it done. When I went back to pick it up, the owner was there. He looked at the work order and said, "Beaton Tulk? You're the politician, right?" I admitted that I was, wondering at the time, I suppose, if that would jack up the price.

"You were a friend of Clarence Chaulk, weren't you?"

"Yes," I said, wondering if Clarence had inadvertently left an invoice unpaid.

He told me that Clarence had never been a minute late with paying a bill, had given him a lot of work, and he loved doing business with him. He praised him to the highest.

"You could send him any size of an order, big or small, and not worry. You'd have your money within thirty days.

"Any friend of Clarence Chaulk can have this work done for nothing," he said as he handed me the shield. And he wouldn't take my money.

That's the kind of relationship I had with Clarence, too. I'd go to bat for him any time because his word was as good as—no, it was better than—cash.

Clarence was only forty-seven when he died in 2001. He packed more into that short time than most people could in two lifetimes. I know I've said a lot about Clarence here, but he was an exceptional guy—way smarter in his chosen field than I was in mine. If any of his family ever get to read this, I want them to know how highly I regarded him. I loved him like the brother that I never had.

A few years after I sold out my interest in Northeast Ltd. to Clarence Chaulk, I put a few dollars into a lobster enterprise in PEI. I'd met a couple of guys, Hughie St. Croix and Harold Trenholm, while I was doing rural development, and we bought an old closed plant from the PEI government.

Hughie had been VP of United Maritime Fishermen (UMF) and has served two stints, I believe, as CEO of the Fogo Island Co-operative.

I think I first met him during the big sealing debate that was on the go in St. Anthony. UMF had been involved in that. It was in Gander, though, and of all places a public washroom, where we literally bumped into each other. Hughie was a smart guy and totally dedicated to rural development in Newfoundland. He and I became lifelong friends. I was saddened when he passed away but proud to be a pallbearer at his funeral.

Harold had been with UMF as well, and we were friends. Harold was from a little community near Cape Tormentine, NB, where the ferry used to go across to Borden, PEI.

Anyway, we bought this old plant situated on the Queen's Wharf in Summerside. We were only at that a couple of years when the floor fell out and into the harbour.

That pretty well killed that venture. This ended my direct involvement as an investor in businesses. My future involvement with businesses would be on behalf of the Newfoundland government when I was minister of Development and Rural Renewal.

4

MHA Fogo District:
My First Term, 1979–1982

THE LEAD-IN TO POLITICS

Politics was always an important subject around our house. If my mother was talking, it was more likely to be of God and religion. If it was my father, then it was most often politics—especially Sunday mornings when Uncle Will showed up. Dad was considered a bit of a guru about politics. Others asked, and seemed to respect, his opinion.

If he wasn't a Liberal before Confederation, he certainly was during the fight for it—and for the rest of his life. It was like a religion to him. He knew what our Newfoundland people went through before we joined Canada.

I've mentioned how he went to work at the age of fourteen in Millertown and the deprivation they went through working in the woods—cutting your own spruce boughs to sleep on at night, working sun-up to sunset, living on baked beans, making ninety cents a cord for cutting pulp—and the first ninety cents each day taken back for that day's room and board. Meanwhile, the owners were getting rich on the indentured service, or slavery—however you care to term it—of the workers.

When Joey started fighting for something better for Newfoundland, my father, like thousands of others, jumped on board.

Who wouldn't? The Water Street merchants, that's who. As a group, they were anti-confederate. They wanted no change, fearing they would lose some of their grip on the economy and on the people.

Out around the bay, though, the sentiment was quite different. There weren't many in Ladle Cove on welfare because we had good soil for growing vegetables, kept animals, and could go at the fish. Still, it was a full-time struggle for many. Dad used to tell the story of an old lady—a widow who was given $13 a quarter—$52 a *year* to live on—by the old Commission of Government of the day. He knew her name, but out of respect for her, he'd never use it. When he spoke of her, he got emotional. He told us, "She starved to death."

He never got into politics himself, but he preached it in every store and stage. As far as he was concerned, Joey Smallwood saved us from all that. Dad and his friend also looked after the voting booth on election day. Naturally, a lot of this rubbed off on me. By the time I went to university in the 1960s, Joey had been premier for a good few years. In university you get exposed to people with all kinds of ideas and beliefs, and there was an undercurrent of change happening.

There's an old saying that goes, "Friends come and go, but enemies accumulate," and that's very true in politics as well. Joey's enemy list started to grow. I began to be influenced by the thinking that Joey had been there long enough and it was time for a change. Smallwood, by then, was considered part of the "establishment," and in university there is always a fomenting of rebellion against establishment figures.

When I got back to Ladle Cove from university in the fall of 1971, Frank Moores was running for premier as leader of the Progressive Conservative Party. I was teaching at the Carmanville school at that time. I guess the Conservatives had heard somewhere that I might be changing my colours, so John Crosbie came to see me.

John had run against Joey for the leadership of the Liberal Party in the convention of November 1, 1969, and had lost to him. (I had supported Alex Hickman, who came in third, although I did no active campaigning for him.) Subsequently, John crossed the floor to the Progressive Conservatives. I told John that I would work for the PCs until Joey was gone, and then I would revert back to my Liberalism.

I was a little cocky in those days, and I told him that I was not doing it because he came to see me, but because I believed that Joey's time had run its course. So I did some work for them in the fall of 1971. My father found out about it, of course. Every evening on the way home from school I'd go past my parents' house, and I always stopped in to say hello before going home.

Dad was sitting at the end of the table having a cup of tea and a smoke when I walked in one day. The first words out of his mouth were, "What's this I hear?"

"What do you mean? What do you hear?"

"Are you working for the PC Party?"

"Yes," I said, "I'm working for the PCs."

He proceeded to tell me, in no uncertain terms, how ungrateful I was. He wasn't even sure I was his son. I was welcome to come there anytime because he was sure I was my mother's son! Dad was really angry. He told me not to come in through the door talking politics.

"Yes," he told me, "you have a lot of book learning and a university degree, but like the rest of them, you have no common sense. You didn't go through what I had to go through, rearing you up, because the days were getting better, thanks to the old gentleman." Joey, of course, was the old gentleman. "And you're out there now trying to put him out of office. Where is your gratitude?"

I left the house feeling like two cents, I must say. We didn't talk any more about politics at my parents' house, but I continued to encourage anyone I could influence to vote PC. The PC candidate for that election was Ivan Jesperson, and Captain Earl Winsor was running for the Liberals.

The PCs lost in our district, but the election was much closer than it had ever been there before. They didn't do that well because of me, I might add, but because of the mood for change and the strength of Frank Moores. A number of districts did go PC. And that was the beginning of the end for Joey.

The two parties were almost tied in the House of Assembly, and then some Liberal members crossed the floor. Finally, in January of 1972, if memory serves, Joey resigned the leadership of the party and the premiership.

A convention was called, and Edward Roberts won the leadership, by a large margin, on the first ballot.

Meanwhile, the Leader of the Opposition, Frank Moores, was asked to form a government. He did and became Newfoundland's second premier. Shortly afterwards, he called an election, increased his members, and continued to govern.

I'll never forget a call I got after Joey resigned. I was sitting there watching the news. The phone rang, and it was the skipper—my father.

"I suppose you've heard that the old gentleman resigned?"

"Oh yes, I heard it."

"I suppose now you can be a Liberal again, can you?"

"Yeah, of course. I never intended to be anything else."

"Well, there's a Liberal meeting called for tonight in Carmanville to elect delegates for a leadership convention. Do you want to go?"

"Yes, of course," I replied.

When we arrived there was a good crowd assembled—150–200 people—and when it came time to elect officers for the Fogo District Liberal Association, Dad was quickly on his feet and nominated me for the position of president. It was seconded immediately. I can't remember if anyone else was nominated or whether I won by acclamation.

I believe that in the back of Dad's mind he was thinking, *You've gotten away once, but you're not getting away again.* I was twenty-eight now and remained president of the district association for about seven years, until I was elected as MHA for Fogo, at which time I resigned the presidency of the Fogo district.

The same day that Brian Peckford won the leadership of the PC Party, March 17, 1979, was the day I announced that I was running for the Liberal nomination for Fogo.

By now Ed Roberts was gone from the Liberal leadership. In the 1977 leadership convention he'd led on the first three ballots, but on the fourth ballot, with Steve Neary eliminated, most of Steve's delegates went over to Bill Rowe. Bill Rowe became leader with 439 votes to 376 for Roberts.

Rowe stayed on until May 27, 1979. There was a lot of unrest within the party, as you might expect, with the party fairly evenly split between Rowe and Roberts supporters after the last convention. A large group of people within the party believed that Rowe could not win against the Progressive Conservatives' Brian Peckford in the next election.

Don Jamieson, who was then the regional minister in the Liberal government in Ottawa, was courted to come back to Newfoundland and lead our party.

He came back following Rowe's resignation in the spring of 1979, and the party executive voted and elected Jamieson as leader.

The Liberal Party's slogan in the 1979 election was, "Bring Jamieson home for good." John Crosbie immediately latched on to it and began calling Jamieson "the Ayatollah," as in Ayatollah Khomeini—the religious leader who overthrew the Shah of Iran and took American hostages. Then the PCs started saying, "Bring Don Jamieson home to help Peckford do good."

Don Jamieson was well respected—and yes, well-loved—in the province. If the election had been held the day he came home, I believe he would have won. We had reached the stage, though, where people were starting to think we needed someone younger—someone with more energy and fight. There was a sentiment among many that our people in Ottawa hadn't fought hard enough to get what we needed from Confederation.

There was a trend and increasing pressure at the time to nominate and elect people who were resident in their own districts—people who knew and understood their own areas. I had been president of the local Liberal association for some time—I lived there and was a school principal in the area.

I had carried on with my community work, you might say, and had fought for new schools, better roads, and more for the area—but I had mixed feelings about running for the House of Assembly. I had a young family, I enjoyed my work, I had student loans to pay off, and I had decided earlier that I probably wouldn't run in this election—nor perhaps any election. That all changed when Captain Earl Winsor, our current Liberal member, came to see me.

Earl came to my school, sat across from me at my desk, and told me that he was not going to stay with it much longer. He was the incumbent, but he was from outside the district. He was from Wesleyville. Because I was president of the Fogo District Liberal Association, he wanted to put my name at the top of his nomination papers. He said he *had* to run this time, because we *had* to win the seat!

I believe his plan was to win the seat, hold it—so to speak—and then resign a few months after the election. Then he would take someone like me, someone whom he had "anointed," around the district and *introduce* them to everyone.

"You've got a space there where you want me to sign," I told him. "Well, I won't be signing it today. I want to think about what you just said. You're telling me that without you, neither I nor anybody else can win this seat?" My old ego was starting to kick in. "Without you taking us around *our own* district, we couldn't win it? Well, sir, I have to think about that, and you'll have to wait for a week while I do."

During that week I got together with a few people I knew who were interested in having me run. Among them were: Eric Burry, a good friend of mine from Gander Bay; Ed Mouland from Carmanville; Dave Tulk from Aspen Cove; Frank Blake from Gander Bay; and Bruce Wheaton, the principal from Davidsville school, who was very interested in politics. These people all told me the same thing: "The time is now."

At the end of the week, as I had agreed to, I phoned Captain Winsor and told him that I was running for the nomination. I believe his reply was, "There's likely to be seven or eight running." I told him, "I don't care if there's a hundred. I've made up my mind. I'm running."

The objective now was to sign up as many Liberal supporters as I could before they chose to support someone else and to make sure that they voted on nomination day. A night or two before the nomination day, Captain Winsor decided that he wasn't going to run and withdrew. So, the nomination was going to be between me and another young guy from Tilting, on Fogo Island.

Let me be quick to add that, if Earl had run, he probably would have defeated me. We worked hard signing up supporters. We scared him off,

I believe. He did not want to run the risk of losing the nomination. We always had someone in my campaign who would call in to the Liberal Party of Newfoundland to tell them how well we were doing. If we had fifty supporters signed up, they'd say it was 100. When it got to 200, they'd say it was 400.

They spoke to people at headquarters who we knew would report it to Captain Winsor. Shortly after the word had gotten to him that we had 1,400 signed up (Captain Winsor had eighty-some at the time), he withdrew.

Earl Winsor was well-liked and well respected by the people. You can count me in that group, too, despite our disagreement, and I still felt that way about him until the day he died. He'd been a member of Joey's government before going into federal politics. He did a lot for the people of the south coast of Labrador—and all of Newfoundland. In any event, on nomination day we won with a vote of 982 to 112 for my opponent—if memory serves.

I took a leave of absence from my work. I believe I started it as soon as I decided to seek the nomination, although that's a bit hazy now. We went at it with everything we had. My team was young, and we had the energy and determination to win.

When I ran for the nomination, Bill Rowe was still leader, as I said earlier, but by the time the election was called by Peckford for June 18, the Liberal Party had replaced Rowe with Jamieson.

It was not an easy campaign. Peckford, in the people's minds, embodied the new, youthful, vigorous fighter they thought we needed. Jamieson did get nineteen members elected—I was fortunate enough to be one of them. A number of other districts were close as well.

I think the other reason Jamieson lost the election in 1979 was that he lost his voice. Jamieson was a great speaker—a spellbinder. He could enthrall a room full of people.

He came to several rallies that we held in our district—Musgrave Harbour, Gander Bay, and Carmanville, I believe. I remember one in particular. We had a motorcade and a big rally planned. The guy running the campaign came up to me at the last minute and said, "He's not going to be able to speak." Apparently he had spoken somewhere, in the rain, and had contracted laryngitis.

"What's he doing here, then?" I asked. I meant, of course, that this was the whole purpose of his visit. Jamieson had planned to shake hands with the crowd and have others do the speaking. Jamieson speaking to the people would have had a powerful effect. He was the one we needed speaking. Unfortunately, Jamieson heard what I said.

"Put up the f------ microphone, then," he said. "I'll do my job!" He spoke, but his voice did not have the power, the tone it should have. Again, unfortunately, it contrasted him poorly with Peckford's youth and vigour. It served to underline what the PCs had been preaching—that Don Jamieson was tired and old and that we needed someone younger and able to do battle with Ottawa.

From that point on it became harder to win. We had a first-class organization, though. We knew how to get the people out—to get them to the polls and get them home again. Despite all of that, the night before election day, I don't believe I slept very much.

The good old days of selling your vote for a bottle of rum were nearly over in Newfoundland, and probably elsewhere, by that time. I can say, unequivocally, that I never bribed anyone for their vote, in that election or any thereafter. We used logic and reason and twisted a few arms—metaphorically—but we always ran on the up and up.

In previous elections, when Joey was in, the candidate ran on his coattails. If he was Joey's man, the majority of the people in our riding voted for him automatically. It had changed now, and door-to-door campaigning became much more important. The big rallies were one thing to get a buzz started, but the game was now to be won door to door.

On election day I started visiting the polls, first the ones farthest away—on Fogo Island—and later those closer to home. I visited them all. When the polls closed we were glued to the TV, waiting impatiently for results to come in. We knew early in the evening that I would be in Opposition if I won. It was a bit of a see-saw in my riding. My opponent for the PCs, Wayne Wheaton, ran a good campaign as well. We won the seat by only about 300 votes.

After the election, the elected Liberals met as a caucus in town, and I had to find a place to live. The new House of Assembly was to sit on July 12, and on July 11 we were called to be sworn in as MHAs.

We had some strength in our caucus with veterans like Don Jamieson, Ed Roberts (our House Leader), Steve Neary, Roger Simmons, Bill Rowe, and Rod Moores. The rest of us were pretty well rookies.

I remember feeling like a fish out of water—new, naive, and a bit intimidated by the whole thing. I was in awe, of course, of the institution, and, like my first day teaching school, having all kinds of self-doubt. Unlike the first day of teaching school, I was more like the student here. So many newly elected people think they are going to change the world, only to find out that there is a learning process, and it simply takes time to learn the ropes before you can accomplish anything.

So I sat, and listened, and learned. I sent out letters of appreciation to all the people who helped with my campaign and made calls to my constituents. Slowly, you start to understand the process, what the big issues are provincially, what the government's strengths are, and their weaknesses.

I was operating under the assumption, when I went into the House, that if something was needed, it would be done. I soon found out that this was not the case—that the Opposition had no influence over such matters. You could raise the issues, but everything depended on what the government wanted to do. Their agenda, so to speak.

I spent ten years in the Opposition, and indeed it was hard to get things done. A lot of it I couldn't get done until I was a minister on the government side. The House of Assembly is a place that soon makes you humble and makes you appreciate the people who put you there. Until you learn your way around, it can humiliate you quickly.

Question Period is the big thing. You don't ask your first question on your first day in the House, no matter how much you are raring to go. You watch. You have to know what you were doing.

It's decided in caucus, as well, who will ask what questions. You'd better know the answer before you ask the question. You may think you are going to put the minister on the spot, but he or she can reverse that very quickly.

Most ministers were very kind to new members. The worst they are likely to say is, "I know this is the member's first question, so . . ." as opposed to going at you tooth and nail. They know it's a learning process—one they had to go through themselves.

Question Period, of course, is where the news media pick up their sound bites. Being unkind to a new member who is simply trying to get something which his constituents need can turn off a whole lot of people—in a hurry. It doesn't sound good on radio, and it doesn't look good on TV.

The purpose of the Opposition member is to keep the government honest, and of course one of the objectives is to defeat them at the earliest possible opportunity. As Ed Roberts used to say, if you want to get things done, you have to get in power.

Your first question is straightforward and simple. You're trying to set up the minister for the one or two supplementary questions you will add once he or she responds.

If you watched the House of Commons Question Period over the years, you would have to agree that some of the best performers were Newfoundlanders. People like George Baker, Brian Tobin, and John Crosbie were masterful. The House of Assembly here in Newfoundland was full of people like that during my time in politics—members who knew what the minister's response would be and had a biting, cutting supplementary on the tip of their tongue. People who could think on their feet and quickly modify their supplementary questions to maximum effect, depending on the minister's choice of words. Ed Roberts was brilliant. Steve Neary was one of the very best. John Efford was merciless.

In my own case, one of the first controversial questions I asked in the House was of a minister who will go unnamed. I asked him if he had ever interfered with the justice system for one of his constituents. His answer was, "No."

Now, you know that you can't call a judge on behalf of anybody. My supplementary was asking him if he recalled doing that. His response was, "Not that I recall." I stood up again and said, "Yes, you did," and related the incident to him.

At that point he challenged me to repeat it outside the House. Of course, once outside the House of Assembly, your parliamentary privilege is gone, and you are subject to being sued.

But I did it anyway—I repeated the accusation outside the House. That was on a Friday. On Saturday morning, the minister called a press conference to announce that he was going to sue Beaton Tulk.

Believing that I was going to be sued scared me, to be frank. I had no money to fight a suit like that. I could lose my house and all. Monday morning I spoke to Steve Neary, who was already a veteran on these issues, and he told me, "Upstairs I have a desk drawer full of writs. Don't worry about it, b'y."

That emboldened me, and I challenged this minister in the House, that day, to take me to court. He never did, but the damage was done. I knew I was right, and now a whole lot of people knew what I alleged he had done. The fact that he never sued me told the rest of the story.

Opposition experience is a very valuable asset for when you get on the other side of the House. Being opposed to something when in Opposition and then suddenly favouring it when in government can raise a lot of eyebrows. Also, sometimes, even in Opposition, you *must* support legislation—especially when you know it is something that is good for the people.

Another thing you have to remember in Opposition is that you are not going to get as much as you should for your constituents. That's not the way it should be. That's just the way it is. The government-held districts will get the most—the governing party will look after its own first.

You'd better answer the calls of your constituents, and if they have a problem, you'd better work on it. If you can't get the big things done that everybody wants, then you'd better solve as many individual problems for as many individuals as you can.

I'm sure that in my years in Opposition we built up 5,000 or 6,000 files of issues that we worked on for constituents. You are not always successful, but you always try. In Opposition the bureaucrats often pay very little attention to you. When you get on the government side, though, that attitude changes noticeably.

Also, you have to stay very visible in your constituency—visit people, attend community events, be accessible. If not, it will come back to haunt you. It's a lot of hard work—not nearly as glamorous as many outsiders see it.

I believe it was Tip O'Neill, former Speaker of the House in the US, who said, "All politics is local." I used to say, "I have no boss here, just the 10,000 people back in my constituency who elected me." They made you their MHA, and they can break you just as quickly if they think you have become unresponsive or too big for your boots.

In Opposition, each member was given a different department to be spokesman for—and its critic. I believe my first one was Social Services, if I recall correctly. Over time, however, I think I was responsible for pretty well all of them at one time or another.

The legislature is not a place for the faint of heart. It's not easy to effect change, and almost impossible in Opposition. Then there are all those people who think you get into politics for the money.

Some must think that you take money "under the table" for voting a certain way. As far as remuneration goes, I was making more in my teaching position than I made going in as an MHA.

As a supervising principal I was making around $35,000 a year. As a backbencher MHA, I made around $22,000. Then there are also doctors, lawyers, and members of other professions who ran who were, no doubt, making way more than they ever could by being an MHA. Peckford had the salaries raised, though, so it got better, but when I was running it certainly was not to improve my financial well-being.

Of course, to people working for minimum wage, it looks like a lot of money. They don't think about what you have to give up—being away from your family, working in your office, or the House, or back in your constituency office, being on call seven days a week—and having to reapply for your job every time an election is called.

To older people it looked like a lot of money, too. That I understood. Most in my father's generation and before had just scraped by. Times changed. If, however, I had worked all my life in the pulpwoods, like my father did, sun-up to sunset, sick or well, hungry or cold, for ninety cents a cord, I might feel the same way.

At the leadership convention on November 1, 1980, after Don Jamieson's resignation, Len Stirling won by a large margin over Les Thoms. I was appointed party whip during that period. Jim Hodder became House Leader. We went into the next election with Len at the helm.

MY SECOND TERM, 1982–1985

After three years in power, Peckford called an election for April of 1982. He was at the top of his game and riding high in the polls. No one but the premier knows for certain why he or she calls an election. I believe Peckford was looking for a mandate to back him in his fight with Ottawa to get more for Newfoundland and Labrador—particularly on issues like the inshore fishery, and perhaps on matters in relation to offshore oil and the revenues therefrom.

The big issue, though, was the offshore-versus-inshore fishery. Ottawa was approving licences for more and more of the big offshore vessels. Peckford set himself up as the saviour of the small inshore fisherman. The people responded positively, and it was a tough campaign for the Liberals.

In some quarters there was hatred for a person if he was against Peckford. That election was the first time I offered my hand to someone and they refused to shake it. Often they may not agree with you, but they'll shake your hand and wish you well. You might call it disagreeing without being disagreeable. But this guy refused. He'd talk to me but not shake my hand.

We worked hard, though, and my team pulled out all the stops to get me re-elected. Without that, and the work I'd done—constituency work—it would have been worse.

Only nine of us survived that campaign—Ed Roberts, Steve Neary, Wilson Callan, Roger Simmons, Eugene Hiscock, Garfield Warren, James Hodder, Thomas Lush, and me.

That number was reduced to eight when Thomas Lush resigned his seat in September 1983 and we lost his Terra Nova district in a by-election on December 7 to Glenn Greening, a PC.

I narrowly won my own seat with 2,704 votes, against 2,438 for my PC opponent, Manson Sheppard. Two or three of us MHAs got together and rented a place to stay when the House was in session—Jim Hodder being one of them. Of course, when the House was not sitting, we'd move out and go back to our constituencies.

PICKING UP THE PIECES

It was after that election that Len Stirling resigned—he had been personally defeated in his district. Steve Neary was named the interim leader on October 16, 1982. I was appointed Opposition spokesperson on Fisheries. The president of the Liberal Party of Newfoundland and Labrador had served a term and then resigned. I got elected president of the party primarily because no one else would do it! I was probably the first in the province to be an MHA and take on that responsibility at the same time. As a result of holding the office of president, you also automatically sat on the executive of the Liberal Party of Canada. Because of this I met, and had several conversations with, he whom I believe was the best prime minister this country ever had: Pierre Elliott Trudeau.

But for my role as president of the party for Newfoundland back then, there were two people in particular to whom I will forever be thankful for helping get me through the job: Vivian Gulliver, who was secretary of the Liberal Party and who became my secretary later on; and Margaret Warren, who was the vice-president of the Liberal Party of Newfoundland and Labrador at that time. They gave every ounce of their energy to keep us afloat.

Keep in mind that we had been decimated in that election, we were very low in the polls afterward, and we had only an interim leader—whom I want to be quick to add served us well.

We were without any resources at all—almost in the same position that we were years later, after Brian Tobin left to go back to Ottawa and Danny Williams became leader of the PCs. We had no district associations left, no Young Liberals clubs. Political parties rise to power and then slide down the wave, and we were at the very bottom of the trough. We simply had nobody in any organized fashion to run the party at the district level.

Our first step in revitalization of the party was to organize the Young Liberal convention in Gander. John Butt, minister of Environment, and others used to taunt us across the floor of the House about maybe renting a telephone booth to hold the convention. But those two people, Vivian Gulliver and Margaret Warren, worked like troopers to make it a success. We travelled the province searching for and tracking down young people who would be the future of our party.

We found one guy, for example, in Ming's Bight, by the name of Jenkins, through Dave Gilbert. Dave owned Beothuk Ford—and became active within the Liberal Party and gave everything he had to help revive it.

I remember we left on a Friday night to drive down to Ming's Bight to try to get this fellow to join the Liberal Party. We did that to pick up one volunteer! That's how desperate we were to try to save the party—and we did that kind of thing all over the province. One of the Peckford government ministers, John Butt, had stated in the House that we would have to hold the convention in a telephone booth, but we ended up registering about 500 Young Liberals for the convention.

Back in the House, I asked the minister whether he had measured a telephone booth, and did he think it would hold 500 people? At the convention they elected their own association executive. There was a runoff vote for president between two guys—Bill Yetman and Danny Dumaresque. Danny won by two votes.

But I don't want anyone to think that I forget how important those two women, Vivian and Margaret, were to us, and to me personally, in helping rebuild the party. It became a mission, not just a job, for both of those fine women.

In 1984 it became obvious to us that it was time to elect a new and permanent leader for the party. Dave Gilbert started talking to a fellow by the name of Leo Barry—retired judge Leo Barry now—who sat on the other side of the House. He had resigned as Energy minister over a disagreement with Peckford but continued to sit with the party. He was one of the PCs' top guns—a smart, well-liked, and effective guy.

So, Walter Milley, Dave Gilbert, and I met with him several times, at the Holiday Inn, and finally convinced him to cross the floor.

Soon after, on the way back from a retreat at Joe Ghiz's cabin in PEI, I had to do one of the hardest things that I ever had to do in politics. I was sitting with Steve Neary—and I love Steve Neary. Steve turned to me and said, "Beaton, I am ready to announce my bid for the leadership of the party—if you will be my campaign manager."

"Steve, it's not in the cards," I told him.

Steve was a tremendous politician. He was one of the "ragged-arsed artillery," but the people loved him—and he may have been able to win the election. There was a feeling in the party at the time, though, that Steve couldn't win, and what was the point of going through this whole process again if he could not beat Peckford? We'd already decided that Leo Barry was the man to beat him. It was the worst thing I ever had to do, and I'll never forget it. I worshipped Steve. He treated me like a son.

Leo ran in our Liberal leadership convention on October 13, 1984, and won with an overwhelming majority.

Leo Barry got elected to the House in October of 1984. The period between 1984 and the calling of the election in 1985 was probably the most enjoyable time that I spent in the legislature. Leo was effective, particularly on the offshore.

THE KRUGER DEAL

The two biggest bills to come before the House in that time period were Bill 37 and Bill 52, to facilitate the sale of the Corner Brook paper mill. Bowater Pulp and Paper was going to close the mill, calling it unprofitable.

The mill employed a large number of people and was, essentially, Corner Brook's raison d'être. So, the Peckford government had discussions with a Quebec company, Kruger, in an effort to have them open and operate the mill. They then brought two bills before the legislature. Bill 52 was to ratify an agreement for Kruger to take over the mill. We had absolutely no problem with that bill and were as eager as the government to pass it.

However, the Peckford government was attempting to *retroactively* take away the rights that workers had negotiated or been given under the Labour Standards Act in 1978. That was Bill 37. At the same time, there was a case before the Labour Relations Board involving these same rights. Bill 37 would have killed these rights retroactively. That word was the reason for our dissent. In democratic governments, retroactive legislation is a no-no, to be used only in the direst of circumstances. In two of the best speeches I've heard in my years in the legislature, by Edward Roberts and Leo Barry, they clearly took us through the reasons why. Simply put, when a government passes legislation and regulation at any given time, say 1978, the public has a right to expect that right or privilege to remain until the legislation or regulation is changed, say 1984. Here the government was trying to put legislation into effect in 1984 to say that, for the intervening years between 1978 and 1984, that was not the case. As both these gentlemen clearly explained, in a democracy that leads to turmoil and is abhorrent to our democratic system of government. In such a situation, one could never be sure what rights one really had. Maybe next year the government would declare that a right you had been given five years ago was not really given five years ago and you were wrong to have assumed that it was.

The Peckford government was using the guise that the Kruger deal would not go through without Bill 37 being put in place—insisting, on one day, that both had to be passed or the Kruger deal would not go through, and on another day saying that one bill did not depend on the other.

We knew that Kruger had already made a collective agreement with Bowater's workers before they signed the deal and that our opposing the attached Labour Relations Bill would not nix the sale. Leo, as leader, was great in opposing this new labour legislation.

Our caucus led by Leo was determined to have the government withdraw the Labour Relations Bill, if possible. If not, then we would keep the debate on the legislation going as long as possible to cut into their public support in the polls.

The normal process in the House is for all members to speak in various stages of the bill, and then the vote is taken to pass the bill. Of course, with its majority, the government wins eventually.

Oppositions sometimes agree with government legislation and most times agree when minor changes or amendments are put in place. However, when legislation arises that is not obviously, or in the mind of the Opposition, in the best interest of the public, every weapon at your disposal must be used to slow the bill down. Then through the press you hope over a period of time to lower the opinion of government in the minds of the voting public. However, governments try to get bills through with a minimum of debate, *unless* it is raising their popularity because it is in the interest of the people.

A weapon generally used is amendment. Amendments give an Opposition more time to debate and, by extension, more time to inform the public what government is doing. One of these is called the Six Month Hoist, which gives every member a chance to debate the bill for a set period of time. That amendment was the tool used mostly in our legislature and is the one Government House Leaders expect Oppositions to use. That amendment reads, "That this Bill not now be read, but six months hence," and each member would be given a chance to speak once, and then a vote would be taken, which the government would win. The debate would be over. That was the last thing we wanted to happen. We wanted to debate the whole idea of retroactivity contained in Bill 37 until the government, who had vowed that it was too principled to ever use closure, would be forced to do exactly that if they were to get this repugnant piece of legislation.

Closure, legislatively speaking, is a dirty word and is viewed as a strong-arm process by cutting off debate on a bill. It denotes that the government is losing ground on the bill in the court of public opinion. It was evident in the media that that was certainly the case. I believe it was Friday, and we knew "regular" debate would be over on Monday. If we could only use a Six Month Hoist, the debate would be over in a couple of hours on Monday. As House Leader, Leo Barry asked me if I could find any tactic to prolong the debate and force their hand.

A tactic rarely used in our legislature is what is known as a "reasoned amendment." Although I knew it was possible that we would not be allowed to use it on the same bill twice, given the fact that we could find no evidence that it might not be allowed anywhere but in the British House of Commons, I was willing to give it a try. If it was allowed by our Speaker, then the debate could go on forever because there were a hundred reasons why this retroactive bill should not be passed. When the House of Assembly opened for its next sitting on Monday, I arrived with eight or nine amendments prepared and ready to go.

When the debate started on Bill 37, Leo started his remarks and shortly after introduced the first reasoned amendment. The amendment stated that this bill not now be read because this House declares that retroactive legislation is repugnant to the principles of parliamentary democracy.

However, before he got a chance to speak, Bill Marshall was on his feet with a point of order. Before going any further, I have to confess that I like and respect Bill Marshall. I thoroughly enjoyed serving as the Opposition House Leader while he was Government House Leader for the Peckford administration. Rarely was he unprepared.

I believe he fully expected that we would do the normal thing and introduce a Six Month Hoist and was caught off guard for the moment. He used a reference that was not correct while trying to persuade the Speaker that the amendment was out of order. The correct references were farther along in Beauchesne's Parliamentary Rules and Forms.

Now, earlier in the fall session, when I was really green and was in a debate on another question with Marshall, he rose and, as only he could, decided to have a bit of fun at my expense. The gist of his point was that the Book of Rules governing the procedure of the House of Assembly was a big book and I should read it all since the crux of the argument was explained on a page farther along than the page to which I was referring.

Now it was my turn. As soon as he sat down, I was on my feet telling the House that I had noted where he would go and that the correct references that he should have read were a little farther along. I quoted the references.

The Speaker recessed and came back to rule that the motion was in order.

Leo then decided to give his own ribbing to Bill Marshall by telling him what an asset it was to have a House Leader who could even make notes indicating where the Government House Leader could get his references in the parliamentary authorities. Marshall smiled through it all.

I never did get to test my theory on whether the House would have allowed another reasoned amendment. As soon as debate was finished on the first reasoned amendment, the government moved to invoke what is known as the previous question while trying to argue that they had not invoked closure. A rose by any other name would smell the same, as debate had been limited to one Opposition member on the main motion.

Premier Peckford himself moved closure on second reading. So much for principles was the debate put forth by the Opposition, and indeed totally unnecessary, as Bill 37, if dropped, would not have nixed the deal with Kruger. It was retroactively passed to hide the mistake the Moores government had made and hopefully, under the guise of the Kruger deal, negate any responsibility the government might have had to the working people of the province.

Third and final reading of the bill was done under closure in the form of the previous question. Before the vote was taken, we, the Opposition, left the chamber to protest the vote, leaving only the stalwart Steve Neary to see that correct procedures were adhered to in the voting. It was a great learning experience for me. I remember Steve Neary telling the Government House Leader, Bill Marshall, when he got frustrated with our tactic that he had better get prepared to have his Christmas turkey at his desk. We had held the government accountable for some twenty-four to thirty hours of debate and forced them to invoke closure in some form or other on a reprehensible piece of legislation.

Many believed, as we did, that the premier had introduced, unnecessarily, legislation that would cause harm to the common working man. The myth of Peckford's invulnerability was destroyed. This, I believe, carried over into the election period the next spring, which greatly improved our standing in the House.

On March 11, 1985, Brian Peckford called an election for April 2. I ran again, with Leo Barry as our party leader. Leo ran a tremendous campaign, the best one I'd yet seen.

Peckford's support was melting as rapidly as the spring snow which we slogged through during the campaign. Leo Barry had earned respect, and the people were now seeing the Liberal Party as a party ready to govern—with a young, educated, and principled leader ready to lead. The enthusiasm was great, and I believe, to this day, that if the campaign period had been one week longer, Leo would have been the new premier.

My campaign picture, 1985

So, at the end of it there were fifteen of us elected—and a number of others who with a few votes more would have given us the House. We went into the election with five sitting members re-offering—Callan, Barry, Hiscock, Lush, and Tulk. Neary and Roberts had resigned, having decided not to run again. Garfield Warren and James Hodder had defected to the PCs.

With fifteen now instead of five, we were a much stronger caucus, having added some really good people, like David Gilbert, a person who had made himself a wealthy businessman in the auto industry and other very worthwhile investments. He had served his community well as a councillor in the town of Grand Falls–Windsor. Dave had tremendous political sense, which he used to help organize the district associations. He was responsible for bringing new leadership to the Liberal family in the person of Leo Barry, without whom many of us would probably not have gotten elected in 1985.

Winston Baker was a person of tremendous intellect and had served as mayor of Gander before entering provincial politics. Winston had tremendous debating skills, and the skill of disagreeing with a point of view and changing the person with that point of view without offending. He brought skills learned in organizing federal elections for the other half of that family duo—George Baker.

John Efford was a person with tremendous drive and passion for the working people of this province, especially those in the fishery. Again, he was a person with tremendous appeal for organizing people. He became a bulldog in Question Period who made ministers fearful when he rose to ask a question, and you could be sure he was going to be first on the evening news—which is essential to winning in politics.

Chuck Furey was a likeable, well-informed, charming personality who could speak and communicate with the best. On his feet he got your attention when he spoke, not only because of his fluency but because of his credible articulation. He was a quick study who had learned politics well as executive assistant to Brian Tobin in federal politics, and he knew the federal political scene well. Chuck showed no mercy when he rose to ask ministers questions in the House, and he analyzed his subject well.

The youngest member ever elected to the House of Assembly, Kevin Aylward took to politics, as we say in Newfoundland and Labrador, like a dog to water. As a young member he had to climb the learning curve and climbed it as fast as anyone I have ever known. Equipped with a bachelor of commerce degree, he was not afraid to ask pertinent financial and economic questions. If he didn't like your answer, his standard response was, "Is that so, now?" In offering his opinion, he would then ask, "Then how about this scenario?" You could be sure that he was about to question the status quo and offer a new perspective. Such an attitude brought a refreshing atmosphere and, if you listened closely, new solutions. His passion and energy were beyond compare.

Roger Simmons had been a long-time member of both the provincial and federal Houses of Parliament. This was not Roger's first time being elected to the House of Assembly. With the exception of Walter Carter and Graham Flight, he probably had more experience than all of us together, having been elected in 1973 and 1975, and elected federally for two terms beginning in 1979.

Roger was just returning home, so to speak, in 1985. However, his return brought a wealth of experience and knowledge to add to the abilities of the caucus. Even though I was not elected until 1979, my recollection of the 1973–1979 period told me that this guy knew how to hold a government accountable for its actions. That period in and of itself had seen some of the toughest times in Newfoundland and Labrador politics. Roger soon proved himself to be a pro.

Chris Decker (now deceased) had been a United Church minister and businessman. He brought a tough and unorthodox way to politics. He seemed afraid of nothing and had a unique way of disagreeing with people just to see where they really stood. If he was satisfied with your argument, he could readily agree by just saying "I suppose." When it came time to decide on an issue, he was as tough as nails but never forgot the people who elected him. If it affected them, it affected him. Talented as a politician, I believe he became the first non-lawyer to become the minister of Justice and Attorney General. His strength in caucus was obvious.

What can you say about Walter Carter? He was the penultimate politician. He had gotten elected under the banners of both the Liberal and Progressive Conservative parties. He has the distinction of having served under three premiers—two Progressive Conservatives and one Liberal—as the minister of Fisheries. Not only is this a record unlikely to be broken anytime soon, it also speaks to the abilities of the person in a particular portfolio. Some might say he was an opportunist. If he was, he would not have been the first, either inside or outside of politics. I found Walter to be completely the opposite. If Carter strongly believed in a cause, party didn't matter. His greatest strength was probably his ability to discern what goals were possible and those that were not.

Again, Carter was not a new politician, but he brought a wealth of information and experience to the caucus.

One of Walter's best characteristics was his great sense of humour. Also, he had a unique ability to use it when it was needed. There were often times in caucus when discussions would become quite heated. Then along came a "story" from Carter. When he was finished, the tensions were gone and civility returned.

A Liberal through and through, Graham Flight, like Roger Simmons, was returning home. Graham never accepted anything because somebody who was supposed to know proclaimed it. Everything was questionable, and if he had an opinion, he was like a dog with a bone. He wasn't giving it up until somebody convinced him it was not a bone or there was a better bone in sight. There can be no doubt that he was on the side of the working person and a Newfoundlander and Labradorian first. That he would fight for what he believed was right was a certainty.

When he returned to caucus in 1985, his experience of questioning proclamations by the all-knowing, and constantly seeking the truth regardless of the authority, helped weld a much more aware group.

Jim Kelland (deceased) was the first mayor of the amalgamated town of Happy Valley–Goose Bay in 1974. That he was the voice of Labrador and brought its concerns to the fore in caucus, there can be no doubt. I knew him for quite some time before the election. During a visit to Goose Bay with Steve Neary, Jim took us on a tour, and we could feel his concern for the area. It was therefore not surprising when he ran for the seat in 1984. He had the intellect and experience to make him a valued member of our new caucus.

We had now reached the point where the party which had been out of power since 1971–72 and almost wiped out in 1982 was on its way back. The Liberal Party's desire to win was alive and well. If the mark of a good Opposition is not only to oppose but possess the ability to govern, then we were it.

We were a government in waiting. Of that there seemed to be no doubt. But time would show the scent would come off the rose and the road to 1989 still had quite a few hills to climb. There was no doubt among us the mistakes and arrogance of the Peckford government would be exploited, and the lessening of their popularity was certain. The talent and desire was in our team to make it happen.

THE SPRUNG GREENHOUSE

The "new" Peckford administration was a weakened government. They had lost a great deal of support all across the province. Then came the Sprung Greenhouse fiasco. Philip Sprung, an Alberta entrepreneur, had the idea for a hydroponic greenhouse that could supply Newfoundland consumers with lettuce, cucumbers, and other delicate vegetables at a reasonable price.

In 1987 the Peckford government reached a deal with Sprung to build this massive structure in Mount Pearl. It became one of the hottest political issues that ever took place in Newfoundland and Labrador. Brian Peckford had a concern, like the premiers before him, with creating jobs—and that's always a worthy goal. There were a couple of factors, though, that contributed to the dominance of this issue and established it so firmly in the psyche of Newfoundlanders and, of course, the House of Assembly.

First of all, it was set up in the Mount Pearl–St. John's area, when there were many other places where there was a more dire need for jobs. If you were living in the metropolitan area, you could not miss, or forget, the big orange glow on the horizon. Had it been established elsewhere, it might have received much less publicity when it failed—like a number of other initiatives by various governments had done before. Secondly, it soon became obvious that the government had not done its due diligence on viability, marketing studies, budgeting, and just about everything else.

It did not get proper debate in the legislature. By the time we got it in the House, it was a done deal.

These factors helped provide the kind of issue that was fodder, if you will, to the Opposition for attacking the government. The media, of course, had very little travel to do to find tomorrow's lead story—they had only to go out their door and look toward the horizon.

Peckford had put a great deal of his "political capital" into the issue—not to mention $20 million or more of the people's money. I wouldn't be surprised if it played a big role in his decision to later resign. It most certainly played a big part in the Liberals winning the next election, and we pounded them every day.

LEO BARRY LOSES CAUCUS CONFIDENCE

Then the next calamity befell us, the Liberal Party—Leo Barry lost the confidence of his caucus. Things seemed to go well until late 1986. The Leo Barry I knew from 1984 onwards changed. I don't know what happened. There are a lot of theories. There was a lot of stress. Perhaps he just got tired of it. He seemed to lose interest. He was a changed man, and not for the better.

Part of my job as Opposition House Leader—on days the House was sitting—was to get us ready for the all-important Question Period. Also, I had to decide who was going to ask which questions and to make sure we were asking the right ones. John Efford was, and I say this without question, the best at asking questions. He knew what to say, how to say it, and he was ready with the supplementaries that would get under the ministers' skins.

We had Chuck Furey, who was one of the best speakers you were going to find in the province. We had Kevin Aylward, Roger Simmons, and others who really knew what they were doing.

The House opened at 2:00 p.m. Monday to Thursday and 10:00 a.m. on Fridays. If the House opened at two, we'd go into caucus at 12:30 to plan our attack. For whatever reason—and I still don't know why—Leo, our leader, started showing up about fifteen or twenty minutes before we had to go into the House, and he'd come in with his lunch on a tray! Like he was a guest—an observer—not a participant.

He seemed to have a lack of interest in what his caucus was doing. That came across as arrogance. There was also some resentment that Leo had been plucked from the PC Party and handed the leadership. Some of our members may have had their own agenda as well.

I tried to carry the load as much as I could, but there was a lot of grumbling in caucus, and some were getting very impatient with Leo and becoming vocal about it. This spread to the party in general, and the media were picking up on it.

In early 1986 there was a Liberal convention where some questions were raised about Leo's leadership. At the first convention after an election, the question had to be asked: "Are you satisfied with the leadership?" Leo had brought the party from five to fifteen members in the House of Assembly, so in normal times a motion for a leadership review would have been turned aside.

We ended up with a vote anyway. Through my efforts, Dave Gilbert's, and others', we set out to try to get an overwhelming vote of support. We needed to stay united if we hoped to form government. Leo came out of it with a vote of eighty-two per cent support.

We went through the summer, but still the grumblings were there. Leo still seemed disinterested. The behavioural patterns remained. He still arrived at caucus a few minutes before we were to go in the House, with a banana, a diet 7 Up, and a sandwich on his tray, and proceeded to have his lunch while the rest of us tried to bring him up to date, and then we had to make a mad dash for the opening of the House.

In December of 1986, there was a by-election. Rex Murphy, who was well-known to Newfoundlanders then—and still is—offered for the Liberals. I ran his campaign. Before that, he had been Leo's executive assistant. Shannie Duff offered for the PCs, and Eugene Long stood for the NDP. There was a lot of discontent out there. People weren't happy with Leo's leadership—his vote of confidence was believed to have been largely "contrived."

The district, St. John's East, was traditionally Tory as well. As Rex used to say, if your blood is red in St. John's East, you are cast into utter darkness. In any event, we succeeded in defeating Shannie, but we didn't win.

The votes left Shannie, but they didn't come to us. They went to Eugene Long and the NDP. When you're unhappy with the government and don't think the Opposition is ready to lead, sometimes you "park" your vote with the NDP.

Another good example of that is the 2015 federal election, when Tom Mulcair and the NDP were way ahead at the start. People wanted to get rid of Stephen Harper and the Conservatives, but many didn't think Justin Trudeau of the Liberals was ready to lead. Trudeau, of course, proved himself on the campaign trail, and the NDP support vanished.

The NDP came up the middle in the election in St. John's East and won the seat. Rex came in third. I remember Rex commenting on that election a few years later at a Canadian Parks and Recreation Association meeting. I was a minister in the Liberal government then and brought greetings on behalf of the government. Rex was the after-dinner speaker. I mentioned during my talk that I had run an election campaign for Rex. When Rex got up to speak, he acknowledged that, thanked me for my efforts, and said, "I came in fourth."

There were a lot of laughs and then a moment of silence, as many knew there were only three contestants. "At the time," he told the group, "there was a very successful real estate salesman who had a lot of lawn signs around, and when the votes were counted, so many people had written in Tony Murray on their ballots that he came in third and I came in fourth."

In any event, that's when the frustration with Leo came to a head. The day after the by-election, I went up to our Liberal headquarters on Church Hill to help Margaret Warren and some others clean up the place and cry in our beer, so to speak.

While I was there I was told of a meeting of several caucus members over at the Hotel St. John's and was asked was I going to it. I said no, as I had known nothing about it. I decided that I should be there, though, so I went.

I hadn't been invited because I was perceived to be "close to him," as Opposition House Leader, and the meeting was being held to find a way to "dump" Leo. Over half of the caucus was there. I sat quietly for a while. There was discussion on openly stating that we had lost confidence in our leader. I told them that we just couldn't do it that way. We needed to call a complete caucus meeting—with Leo there—and make our feelings known. We needed to try to get him to change his ways and try to mend some fences first.

A caucus meeting was called. We went around the table and expressed our concern about how things were going. One member who had been vocal at the Hotel St. John's meeting "passed" when his turn came. When mine came, I told Leo that I agreed things had to change or we had no chance of gaining power in the next election. Leo's response to all of this was defensive. Essentially, he told us, "With or without the fourteen of you, I will be leading the Liberal Party in the next election."

When that statement was made, my heart went down into my boots. I'd been loyal to Leo as Opposition House Leader and had done all I could to make us look united and ready to govern. With that, the caucus meeting ended. Things spiralled downhill from there.

Then Leo went to Boston to a seafood conference, without even the courtesy of telling anyone he was going. The House Leader is supposed to be kept informed, as he or she is in charge when the leader is away. Someone asked me in the House where he was, and I didn't know. Of course, this got out to the news media, and I suspect one of the guys who was really gunning to dump Leo was leaking information to them.

This incident took too much time and energy in our caucus meetings, and when we broke, the press was always there asking the same questions. Then one day in caucus, someone turned to me and said, "We haven't asked our House Leader where he stands on this." I had to make a decision. I could see no way out.

I wasn't prepared to tear the party apart for any leader. When a leader has lost the confidence of his caucus, there is really only one thing you can do. It was a hard thing for me to do, because I believed that if he had put his all into the job, he would be the next premier of the province.

Guys like Dave Gilbert, in particular, and myself included, had worked like Trojans to get Leo to cross the floor, make him leader of our party, and the next premier—and he was blowing it for all of us.

So, Chris Decker, Dave Gilbert, and I were tasked with the responsibility of calling our leader, in Boston, and telling him that the caucus was unanimous in wanting a leadership review. I was the one who pushed the buttons on the telephone to make that call. It was one of the toughest phone calls I've ever had to make, in politics or out. Leo's response was, "You let them hijack the caucus." Leo returned the following day. So, after several meetings of the executive of the Liberal Party, it was decided that a leadership convention would take place.

True to form, Leo, tough as nails, decided he was going to run. He started wearing a pair of red shoes—I suppose he had them specially made—and he started his run to win, or keep, the leadership. I think he believed that we were the rebels and that he had the confidence of the general membership of the Liberal Party.

The leadership convention was called for June 5, 1987. Leo announced, officially, that he was running. He *did* stay in the race for a while. The hopes of finding a good leader, quickly, were slim. Some caucus members were interested, but anyone in the caucus was likely to be viewed as a rebel who participated in a coup to gain power for himself.

That's when Clyde Wells's name started to come up. I believe he was quoted as saying, when he was first approached, that he "Wouldn't touch it (the job) with a ten-foot pole." Clyde was a respected lawyer in St. John's and had been a cabinet minister with Joey Smallwood. He resigned over the bridge-financing of Come By Chance refinery back when John Crosbie crossed the floor to the Conservatives.

Clyde had been president of the Young Liberals. He was a star with the Smallwood government and a well-respected man. Clyde Wells looked like the guy who could lead us out of the wilderness. A number of people went to see him—to persuade him. I did go to see him eventually, although I didn't know him at the time.

So, it wasn't me who convinced him to run. At the time, Clyde was a successful, well-paid lawyer and would have had to take a very large cut in pay in order to become Opposition Leader. We, the Liberal Party, offered to supplement the salary, and finally he agreed to run. Subsequently, Leo Barry dropped out of the race and Clyde won, resoundingly, on the first ballot.

I had a lot of respect for Leo Barry, and I still do, and maybe I could have tried to stop or at least delay the call for a leadership review. It was, however, either Leo Barry or the entire caucus (along with many others in the party) who I had to side with. It was either support Leo, which would blow up the party, so to speak, or go with the majority who were demanding change. I didn't want to see the party go up in a mushroom cloud. Did I feel regrets? You bet I did. Even though I was not the instigator and had no interest in the leadership for myself, I was certainly instrumental in his removal. It felt like a betrayal.

Some of the party membership and the general public supported the move. Others didn't, who had only seen our performance in the House— where we performed well—and were unaware of the leadership crisis in our caucus.

On the other side of the House, Peckford suddenly resigned! I went immediately to Clyde Wells's office, which was next to mine, and told him, "We've just won the next election! Premier Peckford has resigned!"

When Brian Peckford came into the House in 1979, he was as vibrant as any politician I've ever met. By the time he resigned, he was worn out. It might have been the fights with Ottawa, the Kruger deal, the Sprung fiasco, or a combination of those and other factors, but he was worn out. He'd had enough. Subsequently, the PCs chose Tom Rideout as their leader, and immediately we, the Opposition Liberals, challenged him to open the House.

We had twenty-one points over which we wanted to challenge the government. He was not ready. We thought he would wait until fall to open the House or call a fall election. We would have the summer to work in our districts. He surprised us by calling an election right away.

In the election called for April 20, 1989, Tom Rideout lost the government to the Liberals by thirty-one to twenty-one seats. He had been premier for only forty-nine days.

SADIE TULK—MY MOTHER

While this appears to be relegated to a footnote in this period of my life, let me assure you that it is not. On August 8, 1986, my mother died of cancer at the age of seventy-one. She was a guiding light through the first forty-odd years of my life. She kept the family fed, clothed, and loved while Dad was away, for months at a time, working in the pulpwoods.

It was heartbreaking to see her decline at such a relatively young age from the terrible scourge that is cancer. I drove her to the hospital for treatments whenever I could. I remember one trip in particular.

I was driving the old Ford, heading back to Ladle Cove, and likely exceeding the posted speed limit. I saw a big oil truck coming toward me but didn't notice the RCMP cruiser tucked in behind it. The Mountie turned around, came back, and pulled me over. I explained that my mother was in the back seat and I was bringing her back from the hospital. He was chastising me, and I was using all the charm I could muster in order to avoid a speeding ticket. Then, from the back seat came my mother's voice.

"I'm after telling him all day about driving too fast, and he deserves a fine!"

The officer looked back at her, paused for a moment, and said, "No, Mrs. Tulk, since you are with him, I'll just give him a warning."

Recently I was introduced to this man, this police officer whom I hadn't seen in many years, and he said to me, "I know you already. You're the guy whose mother saved him from a speeding ticket."

That was my mother: outspoken, honest, and gone to her reward. I loved her dearly and miss her every day.

5

Four Years in the Wilderness

PERSONAL DEFEAT

In my own district I was seen by many—being the Opposition House Leader—as the hatchetman who had gotten rid of Leo. In the minds of many of my strongest supporters, it was out of character for me.

Not only was I defeated, but our new leader, Clyde Wells, went down to defeat as well. He had chosen to run against Lynn Verge—a strong candidate for the PCs who was well-known and respected in Humber East district. This was the area that Clyde was originally from, and he wanted to represent it in the House.

Clyde had spent the whole election campaigning across the province for his party, and he simply could not spend enough time at it. But he was not a natural-born politician. While he was trusted and respected, he lacked personal charisma and was awkward at the "glad-handing" and small talk necessary to touch people on an individual basis.

I rate Clyde Wells very highly. As a leader, he was top-notch. Within days of the election, Eddie Joyce, who won his seat in the district of Bay of Islands, resigned to make way for Clyde to get into the House. Clyde won that contest.

So we, the Liberals, were finally in, and I'd struck out! I make no excuses for losing. In baseball, a .350 batting average is considered excellent. In politics, even if you hit a home run three times out of four "at bat," you're a loser. You are judged by your last "at bat." In the months following the election, I was devastated.

My district had been in Opposition for eighteen years, had gotten nothing from the governments of the day, and there I was, after ten years as its member, with a good chance to become a cabinet minister and get some things badly needed in my area, and I was defeated.

While I make no excuses, there are some reasons why I believe I lost the election.

First, I think a lot of people in my district considered me a traitor because of the Leo Barry fiasco. This was not the Beaton Tulk they grew up with and knew all their lives. Some believed that politics had changed me—that it had made me cold and calculating.

Secondly, in trying to rebuild the Liberal Party, I had spent a huge amount of time going around the province, organizing, "preaching," and strengthening the party. I was away from my district. Although I had capable people answering my phone, the voter wants to hear your voice, to get your personal commitment. I'd always been a guy that anyone could call, and I'd get right on the issue. Also, constituents—in provincial districts, not so much in federal ridings—expect to see their member in their riding when the House is not sitting. I was spread too thin.

Thirdly, eight days into the election, the PCs had no one to run for them, and I was going to win by acclamation!

Then a fellow named Sam Winsor, a schoolteacher in the district—who, as a matter of fact, I had hired when I was supervising principal there—and a good teacher, too, agreed to let his name stand. Thirteen days later he was the MHA. So, I guess you could say we were caught a little off guard.

Fourthly, there were two stadiums needed in my district. Fogo Island needed one, and so did Wesleyville. The PCs put out the rumour that I was supporting the one for Wesleyville, so that the people along the shore near my home could use it—and Fogo Island was going to be left out in the cold. Not only was that false rumour circulated, but a "letter" backing it up made its way onto the scene.

It was a lie. I didn't catch it in time. It was only the night before election day that I found a letter I'd received from John Butt, PC minister of Recreation, saying, "Thank you for your support of the Stadium for Fogo." I got my letter circulated that night, but it was too late. It was in time to save me some votes on Fogo Island, but not enough. Without it I would have lost the election by 1,000 votes. The final tally was Winsor 2,966, Tulk 2,872. I lost by only ninety-four votes.

We thought about challenging the election results and began the legal process to do so. We believed that there was enough evidence of wrongdoing and that the false letter had swayed enough votes to cost us the seat. It would have been enough to contravene the Elections Act.

But after some considerable thought and soul-searching, I decided to drop the action. Any way I looked at it, there was no upside for the party, the people of Fogo Island, or for me. The suit would have caused a tremendous uproar on Fogo, tearing families apart and dividing other folks from each other. It would have been a no-win victory, and I would have been the fall guy for raising the matter in an open court. It would have also ensured my defeat in any subsequent election, should I choose to run again.

So, I went to see my lawyer, who was George Furey—now Speaker of the Senate in Ottawa—and told him how I felt, and we dropped the case. I was still in a state of anger, of disbelief, of frustration.

For several months I did nothing. A friend of mine in private business, Hughie St. Croix, and I spent the summer contemplating my next move. He had just lost his position as well, as a result of the bankruptcy of his employer.

DEPARTMENT OF SOCIAL SERVICES

In 1990 I was appointed as the assistant deputy minister of the Department of Social Services, Child and Youth Services Division.

With my background in the teaching profession, I had a great deal of experience in working with youth. I'd seen the good, the bad, and the ugly, you might say. In those small rural schools you were part teacher, part social worker, part counsellor, and often a surrogate parent as well. Still, I was unprepared for what was ahead.

One of the chief areas of Child and Youth Services was dealing with youth penal institutions—reform schools, if you will—like the one that used to operate in Whitbourne. It was an eye-opener for me to see some of the terrible things that were going on around the province. I never got hardened to it.

There was a name put on children who ran away from these institutions. They were called "runners." I remember one Friday evening I was getting ready to go out to my home—there was a guy waiting for me—and a call came in from the director of Child Welfare saying that this child—a girl—was a runner and she had disappeared from one of these institutions in St. John's.

It was one of those kinds of evenings. I looked out through the window and it was starting to snow—wet snow—and we all knew that this girl was outdoors and that she was in real trouble, in terms of the weather, in terms of even surviving for the night. So I put my trip off. I told the other guy to go on without me.

We contacted NTV, got her picture put up on the air, and called the RNC, who began a search. Later that evening they found her in a home up in the west end of St. John's or in Mount Pearl, in a private home with no telephone. While the cops went out to their car to call in that they had found her, she disappeared again.

They searched once more. Eventually they found her again. She was termed a runner, but why was she running? Here was her problem. She was a girl who had been sexually abused—by her own father. Her father had been charged and convicted. Her family tried to blame the abuse on her, which is often the case in child sexual abuse cases. The father had just been released from prison, and she was afraid that he would come and get her and attack her again. She believed that no one would protect her.

I remember another girl, who came from a "good" home, well-educated and well-to-do parents, and she too was being abused. I won't go into any detail, and like the previous incident, I will not identify her or her family.

Her story, too, was gut-wrenching. We got her into a group home, and like the other girl, she got counselling. She didn't want to report her family and have them charged because she was afraid they would start abusing her brother to get even with her.

Another child, this time a boy, had a tough story, too. His father had died, and some time later his mother took up with a new partner. In this instance the "stepfather" treated him well, and the boy grew to love him. He lost this second father figure in his life when the man fell out of a boat and drowned. The boy exploded. He just went crazy.

He didn't want to get close to anyone again. He didn't believe any good would ever come to him if he stayed. He lost his self-esteem. I went to see him down at the institution, the boys' home. I had lunch with him and sat next to this frail young boy. He was put under guard for a while. They had to put two people outside his door, for fear he might run or try to harm himself.

So, those were some of the things I saw in that position. It was not easy. One thing I did learn was that societal problems and child abuse know no social or economic boundaries. They happen with the poor and uneducated, and they happen with the rich and accomplished as well. There was another incident that happened during the time I was there, and while it didn't involve kids, it was unpleasant as well.

There were some jobs advertised for the position of guardian at the boys' homes—for Whitbourne and the one down in Pleasantville. One of the applicants said to the interviewer, "I know the people in this department, and I know I'm going to get this job because I've been given the questions for the interview."

This later became a public issue, and there was an inquiry—the Steele Inquiry—to deal with it. This inquiry happened after my time there. I had resigned some time earlier and started working with Investors Group and invested with a couple of friends, Hughie St. Croix and Harold Trenholm, in a lobster plant in PEI.

When I was there, though, I had been asked by the minister and the deputy minister to get this hiring done, so I had a copy of the questions. It was intimated—there was some talk—that I had seen to it that this fellow was given the questions. I knew the fellow. He was not a friend of mine—he was a friend of the minister—but I did not give him the questions.

But when the report came out, it said "the accused," who was the executive assistant to the minister of Social Services—accused of giving the questions to the applicant—couldn't have acted alone, as he had no access to the list of questions. The judge was told that the list of questions was on my desk, marked "confidential." So, of course I had them, because I was about to have the interviews conducted—but I didn't give them to anyone.

There are those who still believe, I'm sure, that I was the one who leaked the questions. First of all, my job had been a patronage appointment, and I was a former politician, so that alone would make me suspect in some people's minds.

While I was in the assistant deputy minister role, I had taken a stockbroker's course, as I knew I did not want to remain as a civil servant. The financial field seemed like it might be interesting. Also, I knew a lot of people who could become prospective clients. I started out with Investors Group, but secretly, I guess you could say, I missed the House of Assembly. I soon began thinking about running in the next election.

FINDING MY WAY BACK

Sam Winsor was our member now—but we were still an Opposition district. Liberal Clyde Wells was the premier, and not having elected a Liberal member, we continued to get nothing. I left my job with Investors Group in December 1992, and in January of 1993 I started working to get the nomination. I talked to the people who had worked with me before and was encouraged to seek the seat again.

I had some strong competition, as there were four of us vying for the position: Harry Hollett, Harold Hayward, John Melindy, and me. There were three nomination meetings held—at Fogo, Musgrave Harbour, and Gander Bay.

When the votes were all counted, I had the nomination. The House was dissolved on April 5 by Premier Wells, and the writ dropped on April

6 for an election to be held on May 3, but I'd already been campaigning hard, long before that writ was dropped. Clyde came into the district for at least one rally—we had several—in Fogo and in Musgrave Harbour and probably another one or two.

I'd made up my mind that this was my last kick at the cat. I would either win and be part of a government that would pay some attention to this long-neglected district, or, if I lost the election, get out of politics for good. I campaigned hard for that election.

On election day I won the seat for the Liberals, with about fifty-four per cent of the vote, against sitting member Sam Winsor for the PCs and Kelly for the NDP. I was on my way back—this time to finally deliver the things my district needed. Or so I thought.

6

MHA Fogo, Bonavista North: Back In, But Out at the Same Time

The Liberals won the election of May 1, 1993, and Clyde Wells remained as premier. Now I was back in the House and on the winning side.

Partway through that term (1993–1996) there was a redistribution of boundaries of the various districts which resulted in the reduction of the total from fifty-two to forty-eight. My old riding virtually disappeared. The change was made to become effective with the next election.

So, while I had been elected in Fogo, it would no longer exist when the next election was called, and I would run again in Bonavista North, which encompassed much of my old district of Fogo.

It became obvious very quickly that I would not make it into cabinet. Why? I didn't know. The day after Clyde had won the leadership in 1987, I had gone to his house and offered my resignation as House Leader. This is traditional, as it is up to the new leader to decide who he will have in which positions.

He had told me that he didn't want my resignation—he wanted me to stay on as House Leader. I stayed as such until the end of that term. But somewhere along the line, between that day in 1987 and May of 1993, when I returned to the House, he had lost confidence in me. I don't know why. I still haven't figured it out.

I didn't get my old job back, and I didn't make it into cabinet. I was relegated to the backbenches. By virtue of that, my participation in the House was minimal. Later on, I was approached by someone from the other side of the House to cross the floor. I told him, "I play for the Montreal Canadiens, and you play for the Toronto Maple Leafs. Win or lose, unless I get traded, I'm sticking with my team."

JAPHET "JAPH" TULK—MY FATHER

I'm sure it was my dad's interest in politics and his belief in social justice that steered me in the direction I took. He died during this tough period in politics for me, on March 24, 1994, at age eighty-three. Now both of my parents were gone.

It is indeed a sobering occasion when you reach the head of your family line. You think about your parents and you say to yourself, "They were two people who did all that they could have with the tools that they had and the time which they were given." You look in the mirror and ask, "Have I?"

SCUFFLES AND SHUFFLES

Partway into that term, on August 26, 1994, Premier Wells made a cabinet shuffle. Gone were people like Graham Flight, Walter Carter, Hubert Kitchen, Patt Cowan, and Tom Lush. These were good people—the stalwarts of the Liberal Party.

Take, for example, Graham Flight. Most people in the province thought he was doing a good job. He had also been very loyal to Mr. Wells—having given up his safe seat to Clyde to get him elected to the House in 1987. Suddenly, the "old guard" was disappearing from positions of influence. This started an unrest in caucus under Wells that hadn't been there before. Some meetings turned acrimonious.

It became obvious that a number of us in caucus were not in sync with many moves that the government was proposing. There was even a movement to force us "on side" or to cross the floor.

I remember telling Premier Wells that he was not just a Conservative but had become what my father would have called a Tory. Of course, "Tory" was not meant as a compliment—especially when said by a fellow Liberal. I also made the point that unless he chose to kick us out of caucus, I and the other "dissidents" would be around long after he was gone.

Along with that shuffle, Premier Wells had taken the Department of Fisheries and rolled it, along with others, into a new department— Fisheries, Food, and Agriculture. I believed, and I still believe, that Fisheries is so important that it must stand alone. I saw this new department as a downgrading of Fisheries. A number of others in caucus agreed.

So, on November 14, 1994, I put forward a private member's motion for Fisheries to have its own department—that the fishery was "the soul" of outport Newfoundland, and that if it (outport Newfoundland) were to survive, then we could not afford to downgrade Fisheries from a stand-alone department.

That resolution was put on the order paper, and I started circulating a petition to get signatures to further this cause. It did get a lot of support, I must say. So, the "rancour" or dissatisfaction in caucus grew. At times Premier Wells could not be sure, when he brought forth a piece of legislation, that the official Opposition and the Liberal dissidents would not combine to defeat it.

In August of 1995, Winston Baker resigned as minister of Finance and president of the Treasury Board. Paul Dicks, who was then Speaker of the House, was moved out and put into Winston's previous roles. That left Speaker of the House vacant. I had already come to the conclusion that I would never be put into cabinet under Premier Wells—or indeed into any other position of influence.

I had made the decision that after this term was served I would not re-offer. I'd serve my term and then get out of politics for good. After all, you get into politics to see some of your ideas used, to effect some positive changes for those who elected you. I'd been stymied in those goals—first by serving in Opposition for ten years, next by seeing our party take power while I cooled my heels outside the House, and then, finally, when all the planets lined up, so to speak, being relegated to a "seat warmer" role.

So, I believed that as long as Clyde Wells was leader, I would be going nowhere—fast—and it looked like he would still be there for the next election. Clyde was a popular leader in the province. He'd stood up along with Manitoba to oppose the Meech Lake Accord.

Meech had been approved in the House by the Peckford government. Wells later sent a letter to Ottawa rescinding the province's agreement. Wells would not agree with the special status "Distinct Society" for Quebec. He became a hero to English-speaking Canada for opposing the Accord and an enemy to the Mulroney PC government and with Quebec for so doing. Later, Elijah Harper played a leading role in turning Manitobans against Meech as well, and without unanimous consent of all provinces, it was never to pass in the House of Commons.

Premier Wells also made a lot of cuts in the civil service and fought with the teachers' unions and others in an effort to keep the debt down in those austere times. Then the closing of the cod fishery—the cod moratorium announced on July 2, 1992, by Ottawa—put 30,000 or more people in Newfoundland out of work. They were tough times, and Wells's approval ratings dropped from seventy-one per cent in April 1991 to fifty-two per cent by November of 1994.

At the time, however, with Dicks moved into Finance and the Speaker position vacant, a strong rumour started circulating that Beaton Tulk would be offered the Speaker's job. First of all, I knew the rules of the house; secondly, I'd been Opposition House Leader; and thirdly, I was told, it was a chance for Mr. Wells to "shut you up!" As Speaker, you don't get involved in debates, and you have little to say in the House of Assembly beyond enforcing the rules.

I didn't believe it. That morning I went on down to the regional office of the federal Fisheries Department regarding a problem that one of my constituents had which involved licensing. Brian Tobin was federal Fisheries minister at the time.

While I was there, my secretary, Vivian Gulliver, called to tell me that I had an appointment at the premier's office at 12:15 p.m. Vivian was also a personal friend and a great prankster, so I thought she was playing a practical joke. "Don't mess around with me," I said with a laugh, and hung up on her.

Ten minutes later she called back. "Beaton, I'm serious. You have to go to the premier's office. You have a meeting with the premier."

I was in my jeans at the time, so I went home and changed into something more suitable for a meeting with the premier. I looked presentable except for a big bandaged finger I'd smacked with the hammer while building a shed that summer.

Anyway, after hearing those rumours, and now with a call for a meeting, obviously I thought he was going to offer me the Speaker's job. It was hard to believe that it would happen, given the differences we'd had. I respected him all the same, and I believed that we could put our differences aside.

I should explain first, though, the chain of command in the Speaker's office: first, Speaker; secondly, Deputy Speaker; and finally, Clerk of the Committees. Each rung down the ladder has less authority and more minor duties. Speaker, though, was a good position. It kept you in the public eye, and to a politician that is important.

So, I showed up in a jovial mood, and Premier Wells was friendly.

The first thing he said was, "What did you do with your finger?" I told him that my mother used to say, "'If you want to get the devil out of your mind, the first thing you should do is to pick up a hammer and saw,' so I did and built a shed."

"Well," he said, "at least you got a shed built. That's more than I got done this summer."

"You said that. I didn't," I replied.

"Sit down," he said, still smiling, and he proceeded to tell me that he had to put Paul Dicks into Finance because he really didn't see anyone else he could put there!

I said, "Well, that's your choice. Obviously, as premier it's your decision who you put where and when."

He then went on to tell me that he was going to fill the Speaker's chair with the current Deputy Speaker and move the Clerk of the Committees to fill the vacant Deputy Speaker's role. By now I was starting to wonder, *Why am I here?*

I thought he was going to say, "You know, Beaton, given the differences we've had, I hope you understand why I'm making these changes and why you aren't part of them." I thought we might move toward a man-to-man, heart-to-heart talk. But I was wrong.

He then proceeded to say, "Given your great knowledge of the House of Assembly, I think you would make a great Clerk of the Committees." You know, we all have egos, but being offered such a junior role, I couldn't take it as anything but an insult. The minute he said that, I saw red—and I don't mean Liberal red.

I told him in words less gentle where he might place the job offer, and then I got up to leave.

"No, no," he said, "come on back."

"No point," I said as I kept walking, and when I was about to go out through the door, he asked, "Can I wish you good luck?"

I turned to face Clyde and said, "Yes, you can—but you're the one that's going to need the luck, not me. I had already made up my mind that I was going to leave the House, and leave you in peace. But you've insulted me, and you've got that northeast blood flowing through my veins again."

I later met some people outside who thought that Clyde and I had made peace, but of course we had not. It went from bad to worse.

As Bill Matthews said to me in jest one day, "If Clyde thought he could get away with it, he'd put you up in the nosebleed section." Meaning the gallery or balcony where visitors sit. So, I just went along with it all and tried to look after my constituents and work out my term.

Then on Thursday, December 14, 1995, Ed Byrne, who was then sitting member for Kilbride, and later became Leader of the Opposition, called Clyde Wells a liar—in the House! Now, you know that's a no-no. It happens on occasion, but when the Speaker asks you to withdraw, you withdraw.

Byrne refused to withdraw. The Speaker can ask you up to three times, and then he "names" you.

Next, the Government House Leader moves a motion to have you expelled from the House. Once you're expelled, you're out for that day. So

Ed Roberts, as Government House Leader, moved the motion, but Byrne refused to leave.

The Speaker then instructed the sergeant-at-arms to move in and expel the member. Normally, one goes out quietly. You are not expected to resist his authority. Not only would Byrne not leave, but other PC members surrounded him to keep the sergeant-at-arms at bay.

The next prescribed step would have been to summon the RNC and have him forcibly removed. But when order was restored, the House continued on with its business and then adjourned for the day, with Byrne still in his seat.

The next day, Friday, December 15, we went back into the House, and it seemed like this thing was going to be swept under the carpet for some reason. Ed Byrne had called the premier a liar in the House and had gotten away with it.

Without rules you have anarchy. It becomes "Do what you want, say what you like, and disrespect the Speaker's rulings."

Dave Gilbert, who was sitting next to me, said, "Beaton, you should give notice of a point of privilege." So I did. I gave notice that I would, after a review of Hansard on the weekend, make my point of privilege on the following Monday.

I researched it on the weekend and made sure I was following the right process, and on Monday I rose to make my point of privilege. The long and short of it was that the police should escort Byrne out of the House—and he'd be out for more than a day.

Ed Byrne accepted the point of privilege, accepted the Speaker's ruling, and left the House voluntarily without the police having to be called. When he left, I withdrew the point of privilege. Clyde Wells came down to thank me later, but I simply brushed him off. "You don't need to be a lawyer to do things like that."

Everyone was satisfied that the decorum of the House had been restored. To tell the truth, I would have done it no matter who it was. Clyde just happened to be the one called a liar. I had nothing against Ed Byrne, either, but the Speaker and every member has to accept that the rules of the House are paramount and must be obeyed.

DIVISIVE ISSUES IN THE HOUSE

A couple of very important issues arose during that term. It was a time of austerity, and Clyde was good with getting "our house in order."

One of the more contentious issues, though, was the future of Newfoundland Hydro. Privatization was proposed in Premier Wells's Crown Speech on February 22, 1994. Newfoundland Hydro was, essentially, the generator of electricity for the province, and Newfoundland Light and Power—a separate entity—was the distributor.

There had been a lot of debate about whether we could privatize Newfoundland Hydro and be better off. Perhaps the sale of it would bring $1.2 billion or so and allow us to pay down our debt and be more solvent as a province. I saw it more as losing control of costs and the consumer having to pay the price in higher rates down the road. Had I been in cabinet, I probably would have had to resign when this issue came up, as I would not have been able to support it.

Premier Wells wanted to privatize it and, in so doing, help to build up—and this was a laudable goal of his—a stronger private sector, which would control rates. The debate went on for some time, in and out of the House. Public hearings were suggested, but Wells refused to hold them. I believe he lost a lot of support over this issue. In the end, the sale didn't happen as too much resistance arose, from a large number of the population.

The other big issue that Clyde Wells undertook to address and resolve was reform of the educational system in Newfoundland. It proved to be as challenging as the Newfoundland Hydro one, if indeed not more. In 1990 he had appointed a Royal Commission to study the operation and efficiency of the school system in the province.

In its report, "Our Children, Our Future," in 1992, the commission recommended a reduced role for the churches in what had been a denominational school system. This system had been in operation before Newfoundland and Labrador joined Canada in 1949 and was, indeed, protected by Term 17, negotiated and agreed to under the Terms of Union with Canada, by both parties to that document.

Subsequent to the release of this report by the Royal Commission, the Wells government and the churches began to negotiate how to implement the commission's recommendations. Talks broke down.

So, in 1995, Clyde Wells put forward a resolution that asked, "Do you support revising Term 17 of the Terms of Union, in the manner proposed by the government, in order to enable reform of the denominational school system?"

Unfortunately, in my opinion, the wording was too vague and the lack of detail was worrisome for a lot of people. After the referendum was conducted on September 5, 1995, the results came back with a 54.9 per cent of the voters in agreement. It was a majority but certainly not an overwhelming wave of support.

On October 13, Premier Wells brought a bill to the House of Assembly which would refer the matter to the federal government in Ottawa for ratification. The bill passed in the House of Assembly and notification sent to Ottawa. That was not the end of the issue, though, and it carried over into the next year and the next government.

But those were the big issues that Mr. Wells had to deal with, and I believe that they took a lot out of him. Clyde was a hard worker. If it meant staying up all night to address something, or to get something ready for the next day, then he was up working. I'd seen a dynamic young Premier Peckford worn down by the burdens of the premiership, and now we were starting to see the same thing happen with Premier Wells.

I believe that he knew there were those among his caucus who would vote against him on certain big issues—the sale of Newfoundland Hydro, for instance. There were those like Walter Noel, for example, who were opposed to the sale and led the call for public hearings. He and I, and a number of other Liberals, would have voted against it.

A defeat on a money bill would be a vote of non-confidence and take down Wells's administration. While a defeat on the Hydro bill would not be a vote of non-confidence, it would have been a major embarrassment

While Clyde was indeed a good leader, he was not a born politician. He had become a national figure over the Meech Lake Accord, but it was not something he wanted. He was later quoted by *Maclean's* magazine as saying, "Anonymity is a wonderful thing. I welcome the return to it." Whether he was tired of it all or simply wanted to go back to private life for his own reasons, I don't know.

In any event, in January of 1996, Clyde resigned as the fifth premier of our province and, in so doing, became the last person to resign as the premier of Newfoundland. All future premiers would resign or leave office as the premier of Newfoundland and Labrador.

Brian Tobin, who, along with Sheila Copps and John Nunziata—the infamous "Rat Pack"—had tormented the previous Progressive Conservative government of Brian Mulroney in Ottawa, and was now federal Fisheries minister in the Liberal government there, ran to replace Clyde Wells. He won the leadership, by acclamation, at the provincial Liberal convention on January 17, 1996. He called an election for February 22, and on February 26 he was sworn in as our sixth premier.

I'm not sure I accomplished anything of importance for the province as a whole during the 1993–1996 term, but the absence of duties in the House of Assembly allowed me time to work more directly on behalf of my constituents. That attention certainly paid off.

The arrival of Tobin brought a fresh approach. I soon changed my mind about running again. I knew I could work with this guy. I wanted, very much, to be part of the Tobin era.

THE TOBIN ERA, 1996–2000: WINDS OF CHANGE

The election of Brian Tobin as party leader on January 17 and our subsequent win in the provincial election on February 22, 1996, gave me a new political life. Although it was the dead of winter, there was a warm breeze blowing across the province, figuratively speaking. The mood had changed. The attitude turned positive.

I had given up hope of any position of authority in the government of Clyde Wells—a position where I could contribute positively to my own constituents or the people of the province at large. I had intended to leave quietly when the next election was called. Tobin changed everything.

On March 14, 1996, in setting up his new cabinet, Tobin appointed me as Government House Leader and minister of Forestry and Agrifoods—which also included Wildlife and Inland Fisheries at that time. Now I had some things to sink my teeth into.

It really underlines the saying that a day is a long time in politics. How quickly things can change. Obviously, Tobin believed in my capabilities. My objective had always been to be a Liberal cabinet minister, where I could influence positive changes—changes that would improve not only the lives of my constituents but also all of rural Newfoundland.

I had no interest in being premier, or in an impotent position such as Opposition member, or a seat warmer on the government side. I didn't go to St. John's because I was merely looking for a steady paycheque. I know it sounds self-serving, but I honestly came to try to make a difference—to effect positive change.

My appointment as Government House Leader was unexpected. We had elected a strong team to the House, and there were a number of others who could have been selected. But my experience as Opposition House Leader from 1984 to 1989 gave me valuable experience, and I had come to know the rules of the House intimately.

This was also a chance to affect the atmosphere in the House, which has a big effect on getting legislation in place in a timely manner. I loved the job! I will be eternally grateful to Mr. Tobin and the people of Bonavista North for the opportunity.

So, on March 28, 1996, six days after the House opened, and seventeen years after my first election to the House in 1979, I took my first question as a cabinet minister. The question came from Paul Shelley, member for Baie Verte–White Bay, who was also Opposition critic for Forestry.

Before I had a chance to respond, Brian Tobin said, "The Member for Bonavista North and minister of Forestry has waited a long time for his first chance to answer a question in the House."

"Not just a long time, Mr. Speaker," I said, "but a *long, long* time."

My first big task in the role of Government House Leader came on May 23, 1996. It was to get unanimous consent in the House on a resolution put forth by Premier Tobin to request that the House of Commons give immediate approval to the resolution on education regarding Term 17, which Clyde Wells had sent to Ottawa. The motion was passed unanimously.

Brian Tobin as he left the premiership in October 2000. His message to me: "Beatie, don't forget to turn out the lights."

It was important to get it done at once, as the Commons was about to adjourn its spring sitting. They did get it done, and the Senate approved it over the summer. Subsequently, however, the Roman Catholic and Pentecostal churches went to court to seek an injunction to stop the revision.

The question had not been as clear as it should have been, so Brian Tobin chose not to fight the injunction. Instead, on July 31, 1997, he proposed a reworded question in a new referendum. The new question was clear, and while it removed the total control of children's education from the hands of the hierarchies of the churches, it specifically allowed the teaching of religion in schools.

That referendum returned a seventy-three per cent vote in favour, and Ottawa agreed to revise Term 17 of the Terms of Union. With that, Newfoundland finally achieved a secular public school system.

Premier Tobin achieved a lot for our province. But if you were to ask me the signature piece of work he got done, this, in my opinion, was it.

STEVE NEARY PASSES

Just after the start of the Term 17 education debate, on June 7, 1996, Premier Tobin rose in the House of Assembly to announce the passing of Steve Neary. I didn't speak, simply because I couldn't. Steve was too close a friend.

He was a man of the people. One of his favourite phrases was "the ragged-arsed artillery," when referring to the common man—and he used it often but with the utmost of respect.

I never got over having to refuse his request, years earlier, to manage his campaign in a proposed run for the Liberal leadership.

At that time we didn't believe he could beat Peckford. A group of us in the "inner circle" were already working to get Leo Barry to cross the floor from the Progressive Conservatives and seek the leadership. Perhaps Steve could have won. Perhaps he could have beaten Peckford and become Liberal premier. I think he understood why I declined, and I believe he accepted it.

With all the people he knew, and who could have been asked, I was honoured and proud to serve as one of the pallbearers at Steve Neary's funeral.

TOBIN'S STYLE

The fight for a secular school system—spearheaded by the Liberal Party under Wells and then successfully completed by Tobin—was to have negative effects on our party for years after.

BEATON TULK with LAURIE BLACKWOOD PIKE

In my opinion, it cost us seats in the next election—seats which we were unable to win back until 2015. But it was the right thing to do. It needed to be done, but that doesn't mean that everyone was happy with it. Just getting Term 17 changed was only the start of it. There were bound to be problems and irritations—bumps in the road—as we proceeded to implement the changes.

Born in Stephenville—almost as far, geographically, from being a townie as one could be in Newfoundland—Brian was as smooth as any big-city lawyer. He studied political science at Memorial University but did not go immediately into politics.

His personality and ability to speak took him first to work as an on-air news person at what is now NTV. Later he honed his skills as executive assistant to Don Jamieson when Mr. Jamieson took over the leadership of the Liberal Party in 1979.

So, he was well-prepared when he ran as the Liberal candidate for MP of the Humber–Port au Port–St. Barbe federal district in 1980 and was elected to the House of Commons. His performance in Opposition as a member of the "Rat Pack" was legendary.

Later, his resolve and ability to fight for a just cause were magnified by his actions as a federal cabinet minister in the so-called "Turbot War," during which a Spanish ship, the *Estai*, was arrested and made an example of for overfishing and using a mesh size illegal in Canada. These actions made international headlines, and Tobin took on hero status among conservationists and those whose very livelihood depended on dwindling fish stocks—especially in rural Newfoundland.

His news conference on a barge near the United Nations in New York harbour is still remembered for his plea to save the "last, lonely, unattractive little turbot, clinging by its fingernails to the Grand Banks."

Tobin had clearly shown when he was in Ottawa that he wasn't afraid to face the tough issues. He was a masterful orator, a convincing speaker. When he sensed resistance from the Opposition, he wasn't afraid to go to the people. He won their support more often than not.

When he came back to Newfoundland to be premier, he understood the province and the feelings of rural Newfoundlanders. He knew how to use drama, but he also knew how to reach consensus or an acceptable compromise in order to get policies put in place.

More than anything, though, I believe he understood the psyche of the rural Newfoundlander. He could see the mood of despair, of anger, of frustration at the loss of the cod fishery. Newfoundlanders needed hope, and he believed that they needed to be totally involved participants in the designing, building, and climbing of a ladder back up to a better life.

WE'RE DOING IT RIGHT HERE

Premier Tobin knew that there was a small group of entrepreneurs spread across the province who could effect change. They had the abilities and the will. He wanted to give them the confidence.

To that end, he first started with a series of television ads with the theme "We're Doing it Right Here." Each ad featured a different Newfoundland entrepreneur, working in his business, creating jobs, and showing his or her confidence in our economy and the future of the province. Waving proudly in the background was the Newfoundland flag. The subliminal message was simple: Not only can you do it, but it's patriotic to do so.

It was a masterful piece of work, and the hope which Tobin had brought was beginning to blend with enthusiasm and the confidence that we could do it ourselves. My work in Forestry, Agrifoods, Wildlife, and Inland Fisheries took me to all parts of the province. Often I met some of those people in the ads and others like them who needed only encouragement to develop a new business or add a new product.

I worked with sawmill operators, outfitters, farmers, and many others who had a dream and a drive to create something new, and in so doing they could help build up the economy of the province. This work was right up my alley. I grew up in a rural area, my family had been involved in forestry, and I understood the drive and the will to succeed that these people had.

I developed the habit of dropping in on some of these entrepreneurs everywhere I went. For example, I stopped one Saturday morning in

Indian Bay to see Gary Collins—who is now an award-winning author—who operated a sawmill there. When I introduced myself, he didn't believe me at first. "Damn you. Don't go tarmentin' me this morning! What would the minister of Forestry be doing stopping by to see my little operation?" he asked.

I finally convinced him that I was not an imposter—and that I was not there to spy on him or to criticize what he was doing, but to find out from him what he needed in order to be more successful. We not only became friends, but I discovered that he had a desire to do new things and create new wood products.

Reg Philpott at Cottle's Island Lumber was the same way. He was an inventive entrepreneur. At one point he prebuilt small houses for Japan. He took Newfoundland hardwoods like birch and turned them into kiln-dried flooring. He later built prefab houses that he shipped down to Chile. There were many others, too, whom I met and worked with along the way.

DORA TULK

On December 31, 1996, I married Dora, who was and is my soulmate. She is kind and generous to a fault—having once given her sister's coat to someone whom she believed needed it worse. (Her own wouldn't fit). Working side by side with me, in politics, she was able to secure much more support than I ever could have by myself.

She is devoted to her family and mine. She is also very forgiving, but don't ever tell her that all politicians are dishonest. If you do, she will take the lumping together of all politicians as calling "my Beatie" a thief. She would defend me with the ferocity of a lioness defending her cub. Dora will do what Dora decides to do. Nothing or no one can stop her.

Dora has two daughters, Alicia and Kerry-Lynn, and three grandchildren: Christopher, Mackenzie, and Samantha. Samantha was always reluctant to leave when she would come to visit us. When she was about eleven years old, she came to live with us permanently. Samantha now has a beautiful little girl by the name of Jayda. Dora's daughters and their partners—Dan and Scott—live in St. John's, so we get to see them, her grandchildren, and our great-grandchild quite often. Great-grandchild? How old do I be?

As people get older, more challenges—not the least of which is health—seem to arise. I can face them all with Dora. The good days are more joyful and the tough more tolerable because of the love of my life.

My wife, Dora

Dora's daughter Alicia Callahan and Dan Best

Left: Alicia's son Christopher Ryan
Right: Alicia's son Mackenzie Ryan

Dora's daughter Kerry-Lynn Callahan and Scott Connolly

Dora's and my granddaughter Samantha
and great-granddaughter, Jayda

OTHER INITIATIVES

We established an Advisory Council on Inland Fish and Wildlife, and on January 28, 1997, we announced the first board.

The next big issue my department addressed was Newfoundland Farm Products (NFP), which was the producer of chicken for the province. NFP had been created twenty or so years before, and it was costing us $7 million a year or more to subsidize the operation. It really should have been a private enterprise. Government doesn't belong in private enterprise.

The initial purpose was to create a poultry industry in Newfoundland and create product here that had previously been imported. There's nothing wrong with the concept, but government should be encouraging private entrepreneurs and creating the right conditions for success, not getting directly involved with a financial stake—the people's money.

So, we started a process to privatize it. The other chicken producers in the province put together a company called Integrated Poultry Ltd. (IPL), and on June 16, 1997, we announced the divestiture of NFP to private enterprise. A couple of weeks later, in a cabinet shuffle, Kevin Aylward assumed the ministry of this department, and it was left to him to complete the process. Kevin has never been afraid to take on a new initiative or correct what is wrong, and so he did with chicken production in this province. Today its success can be largely attributed to this young man.

Another initiative undertaken in the fifteen months that I was responsible for Inland Fisheries and Wildlife was to start a two-year trial test on the Gander River under the Gander River Management Authority (GRMA) to establish a community-based management system of the Gander River salmon fishery. That group had an extra set of licences, over and above the regular provincial ones, which they could sell to raise funds to enable them to manage the salmon stocks on the river. We believed that putting control of this resource in the hands of local people with a vested interest in seeing it preserved was a good way to ensure its survival.

We also put in place an Agrifoods Innovation Program with the goal of encouraging private entrepreneurs to get into products we weren't producing here, but products for which we had the resources here. Take, for example, Rodrigues Wines in Whitbourne. It's very successful in producing a wide variety of wines from berry products which grow in our province. The owners' foresight in gaining the "Kosher" designation has widened the products' appeal and their market. Several other enterprises have now started up in this beverage sector, but Rodrigues was the pioneer.

Another thing we put in place was a twenty-year Forest Management Plan (FMP), which was to be an ecosystem plan as opposed to a timber-supply program. We had resource in the twenty-to-forty-year range as well as the sixty-to-eighty-year range, but little in the forty-to-sixty-year range due to insect infestation and other factors. We undertook to address this problem with a proper plan.

As an interesting side note to this ministry, at least to me, I got to meet Prince Philip, who was the honorary president of the World Wildlife Federation.

PRINCE PHILIP

The Wildlife ministers of the Atlantic provinces were invited to Halifax to have dinner with the Prince. I had the unique experience of being his dinner guest, seated beside him, the next guest being maybe eight feet away.

He was a very interesting, personable guy. After a few sips of wine, the conversation got very relaxed. He's the kind of guy who readily dispenses with protocol and gets down to regular conversation. The "Your Royal Highnesses" and the "Mr. Ministers" soon vanished.

He asked where I was originally from: "Old chap, now where do you hail from?" I told him I came from a small, isolated community on the northeast part of the province—which, when I grew up there, had no electricity, running water, or plumbing, and no roads, and the only access to the outside world was by boat or radio.

Then he became curious. "Where did you take your bath?"

I explained to him the galvanized washtub we used once or twice a week.

"No no," he said, "where did you use the toilet—the john?"

"Oh," I said, "you mean the outhouse."

"Yes," he said, "number nineteen."

"Number nineteen," I asked, "you use number nineteen?" I was confused.

"Yes," he said, smiling, "I've used number nineteen on many occasions in the armed forces."

We talked away for a couple of hours—however long the meal lasted—about everything you can think of, even a bit about wildlife. At about 10:00 p.m. he got up—he knew his schedule—and said, "I have to leave now. I'm the honorary president of WWF, but you're the guy who has to do something about it." With that he was gone, and of course I expected never to talk with him again.

Several weeks later, he and Queen Elizabeth began a royal visit to Newfoundland and other parts of Canada. Premier Tobin and the lieutenant-governor went to meet them at the airport in Torbay. He slid into the seat next to Tobin and said to him, "You have a chap by the name of Tulk working for you, don't you?"

Premier Tobin immediately turned to him and said, "And what has he done now, Your Royal Highness?"

"Oh, nothing," Prince Philip replied. "Nice chap, nice chap."

Later, he walked into the Confederation Building—there was a salute for him outside—and all the cabinet ministers were lined up inside to do the handshakes and curtsies—whatever was the prescribed protocol. When it came my turn, he said, "We're getting together quite often now, aren't we?"

"Yes, Your Royal Highness," said I. The Queen and he then went on in and signed the guest book, and Queen Elizabeth sat in the Speaker's chair. When the procession was coming back out, he turned aside to speak to me. "How are you doing?"

"Fine, Your Royal Highness," I told him. "And how are you enjoying your trip?"

My wife, Dora, and I presenting a painting of the bird sanctuary
at Cape St. Mary's to Prince Philip

"How do I know? I just got here," he said, smiling, and then went on out.

A couple of days later, there was scheduled to be a special presentation to Prince Philip and the Queen. It was a portrait of the bird sanctuary at Cape St. Mary's. I got a call from the premier's office, and apparently Prince Philip's principal secretary had asked that I do the presentation.

"What do you and the prince have going?" Premier Tobin's executive assistant asked.

"Oh, nothing, we're just old buds, that's all," I said with a laugh.

So, Dora and I got all dressed up and went down and did the presentation and had a little chat with him and the Queen. Several days later I got a note from Prince Philip's principal secretary inviting me to the palace if I ever came to London. I never took him up on it, but it was a nice gesture from a man who, although immersed in all the pomp and ceremony, hadn't lost the common touch.

Queen Elizabeth Silver Jubilee medal

JOSEPH KRUGER

Through my work with the Department of Forestry, I got to know Joseph Kruger, owner of the company Kruger Inc., which had bought the Corner Brook mill. He'd been at my office in St. John's, and I'd also met with him in Corner Brook. I dropped in to see him at his office in Montreal on the way to a meeting in Trois-Rivières in early June 1997. He had all his board of directors there. I sat down at the table and Joseph asked, "What can I do for the minister of Forestry of Newfoundland today?"

"Well," I told him, "one thing you could do for me and the sawmill operators in Newfoundland would be to make it possible for them to sell wood chips to you."

At the time, Abitibi Price, which owned the Grand Falls and

Stephenville mills, were the only real market. Getting another buyer would open it up to competition and perhaps improve the price the mill operators could get for this by-product of milling. As it was, Abitibi could almost set its own price, so the mill operators were at the mercy of one company.

He looked across the table and said, "Done."

A couple of the board members started to object. Joseph said, "No, no, no. I asked the minister what I could do for him. He told me. So, we're doing it." He followed through, too, and as a result of that spur-of-the-moment meeting, when I was on my way to another, we managed to get some competition for wood chips. Mill operators across the province began hauling chips to Corner Brook, as well as the other two mills, and started getting more value for their product.

DEPARTMENT OF DEVELOPMENT AND RURAL RENEWAL (D2R2)

I was in Trois-Rivières, Quebec—this was the meeting I was headed to when I stopped in to see Kruger—at an interprovincial agricultural meeting with my deputy minister and our wives. We'd only been there one night when, the next morning, just after the meeting started, Hal Stanley, the deputy minister, whispered to me that I needed to call the premier's office.

Of course, when you are summoned to call the premier, you go, even if you are wondering to yourself, *What the hell has gone wrong that he needs to call me?* I called him. That was the morning of July 3, and Brian Tobin asked, "Where are you?"

I said, "In Trois-Rivières, Quebec."

"Well," he said, "that's a long way from the lieutenant-governor's office in St. John's! Tomorrow you are going to be the minister of the Department of Development and Rural Renewal—being sworn in at 10:30 a.m.—so you'd better get home."

Dora had gone out shopping! I found her, we packed quickly, and Hal Stanley arranged for a taxi to take us to Montreal. As we got close to the city, a police car pulled in front of us—I don't know who arranged that—and escorted us quickly to the airport. We barely made it to our flight and finally got back in St. John's around four o'clock in the morning.

So, later that morning, on July 4, 1997, I was given a new responsibility along with that of Government House Leader. D2R2 was the perfect job for me, no mistake. It's something I'd always wanted to do, and I loved doing it.

Tobin had set up a new approach to economic development in the province—from the "bottom up," instead of the traditional way since Joey's days of "top down." That initiative was launched with the "We're Doing It Right Here" ad campaign.

REGIONAL ECONOMIC DEVELOPMENT BOARDS (REDBs)

Clyde Wells, in fairness to him, had set up an Economic Recovery Commission (ERC), but it wasn't very successful. But one of the recommendations which came out of its report was the idea of setting up Regional Economic Development Boards. Judy Foote—who went on to become a federal cabinet minister and, in 2018, was appointed the first female lieutenant-governor of Newfoundland and Labrador—had the department before me, and she had already made a start on setting up these boards.

My job now in this initiative would be to get the grassroots involved and get these boards up and functioning. The report recommended nineteen boards. We ended up with twenty.

Each regional board would put together a Strategic Economic Development Plan (SEDP) for its area. My job was to encourage and coordinate the setting up of these boards and get them organized and working on their plans.

The idea was to harness the new energy, enthusiasm, and confidence that the "We're Doing It Right Here" program had created and get those people and others involved in a broader vision—for their whole area. All these SEDPs from the twenty economic zones would then be combined into a plan for the province.

To facilitate the enactment of individual initiatives, along with the federal government we set up a Strategic Regional Diversification

Agreement (SRDA), which would provide a certain amount of capital to get projects going. The regional boards would not carry out the initiatives themselves but connect private entrepreneurs and community organizations—the ones that were willing to participate—to government for access to SRDA financial assistance.

A good example of this was the Barbour Premises Committee in Bonavista North, my own riding. Because of the strength of the proposal and its future benefits, it was able to acquire millions of dollars to successfully complete its project. That same REDB supported the development of the Windmill Bight Golf Course.

(On my last day as premier, we awarded them approximately $2 million to build this facility. Later, in 2001, as I left the political scene, the so-called environmentalists who had objected won the day. It was never to be built.)

I remember those two projects in particular because they were in my own riding—but there were numerous others spread across the twenty REDBs in the whole province. Neither I or my department—D2R2— should take credit for the successful projects initiated. That credit belongs to the local REDBs, the entrepreneurs, and committees who got them done. Our job was to encourage and enable.

THE ATLANTIC GROUNDFISH STRATEGY (TAGS)

Most of our activity on the economic development side, provincially, was precipitated by the closing of the groundfish fishery—essentially cod— and was designed to address the devastation, economically, that this had caused the area.

The federal government had set up a program to help in the short term—a program called TAGS (The Atlantic Groundfish Strategy). It was designed to provide funds for retraining, subsidizing incomes, and more for those approximately 30,000 workers who were affected by the closure on July 2, 1992.

Rightly or wrongly, most Newfoundlanders believed that it was the federal government which was responsible for the collapse of the fishery—by granting too many licences and increasing quotas and so on.

I believe likewise. But it was also believed that the stocks would recover quickly. They didn't. The TAGS program, the feds believed, had enough funding to last until 1999. It didn't.

It became obvious in late 1997 that the funding would be depleted by May of 1998. The prime minister and the federal Fisheries minister, David Anderson, recognized this, so they sent down a Commons Fisheries Committee, chaired by Newfoundland MP George Baker, to go around the province for a first-hand look at the severity of the situation.

I had been tasked by the premier to handle this problem—the problem created by the funding gap—and to get a program in place to follow the end of TAGS. The difficulty in trying to get Ottawa's help was a feeling, in certain quarters across the country, that Newfoundland was just a drag on Canada—that things weren't half as bad here as we said they were.

The committee was going only to certain selected areas and was leaving out the northeast part of the province, the coast of Labrador, and the Great Northern Peninsula. I went after them on that, and they got it changed. It also became a somewhat contentious issue that the federal Human Resources Development (HRD) minister was not with them.

After all, the funding, like TAGS, was going to have to come out of his department, not the Department of Fisheries or some other place— and Minister Pierre Pettigrew wasn't there. How could he see, first-hand, the need and develop a response without participating?

The committee was made up of members of all parties in the House of Commons, including the Reform Party, which of course had very little first-hand knowledge of coastal fisheries, especially the Atlantic fishery. It was a way, however, for them to see our situation here and to build a consensus among the different political parties for redress.

At the same time, a memo started circulating, from a company called Merx Consulting, among federal government employees, about how they were going to contend with the "violence and the destruction of property that might ensue"—in Newfoundland and Labrador particularly—when the TAGS program ran out! This memo, of course, became a bone of contention for all politicians in Newfoundland.

This issue was raised first in the media, and then I raised it in the

16

House of Assembly and to the federal government. We all condemned it in the House—this outrageous statement about what they felt might happen. I asked federal HRDC Minister Pettigrew to disown the statement and apologize to Newfoundland and Labrador. All the PCs, the single NDP member, and the Liberals unanimously condemned it.

Some people believe that we in the House of Assembly are like a bunch of youngsters, fighting with each other because we have nothing better to do. When the chips are down, however, *all* members are Newfoundlanders and Labradorians and will come together to fight any unfair characterization or smear on the people of our province.

POST-TAGS

Then we put together an all-party committee to deal with the post-TAGS issue. I introduced a resolution in the House, as Government House Leader, saying that we as a House of Assembly believed that redress of the situation was the responsibility of the federal government: due to its mismanagement of the fishery, 30,000 people would now not only be out of work but out of income of any kind; further, the fishing industry was as important, proportionally, as the forestry industry was to British Columbia, the oil and gas industry was to Alberta, and *twice* as important as the auto industry was to Ontario. So, the committee went to Ottawa to pursue this—to see all the ministers who might be involved in the decision-making process, and to meet with all the leaders of the political parties.

At the same time, there was a book on the market by Michael Harris called *Lament for an Ocean*. It outlined, in the best way I've ever seen, how the cod stocks of Newfoundland and Labrador got destroyed. We bought thirty or forty copies of this book, and as we made our way to the various departments, the various ministers, and the leaders of the political parties, we presented each with a copy of the book. We told them, "If you read this, you will understand what we are talking about."

So, with all this attention—all this pressure put on the federal government—the feds came to understand very quickly that more needed to be done to mitigate the devastation done and correct the shortcomings of the now expired TAGS program. On June 19, a program was announced, and after consultation, a final program was announced on July 27, 1998.

The new program would address early retirement benefits, capacity reduction and licence buyback, income replacement, mobility support, and other issues. We sought $1.2 billion. We got $750 million, much of which went to Newfoundland. This also allowed the province to implement a number of short-term job-creation projects which were to benefit many communities.

THE OUTDOOR RESOURCES COMMITTEE

There was a growing concern in the province that the public resources—the forest, the waterways, game birds, fish, moose, and the wide-open spaces—were moving from public use into private hands to develop jobs. Perhaps our GRMA program for the Gander River caused some of that concern. People were afraid that as we went forward they would lose access to these public lands and resources.

So, I asked Premier Tobin what he thought of me setting up this committee, with some other ministers, and doing a tour around the province. We'd hold public hearings and get the people's opinions and try to allay their fears—which, frankly, were largely unfounded. In keeping with his belief in public consultation, Tobin was all for it.

On September 23, we began hearings which were well-attended and received. We had over ninety written submissions, as well as all the verbal ones, from the eighteen meetings held. We produced a report, a government publication that was entitled "Our Smiling Land: Government's Vision and Declaration of Rights for Outdoor Use in Newfoundland."

We acted on some of the suggestions and complaints immediately. For example, one of the common complaints was that you couldn't use your ATV to retrieve your moose kill. Kevin Aylward, who was then minister of Wildlife, and Ernie McLean, who was the minister of Public Services, put in place a rule that allowed a hunter to make five trips by ATV to retrieve his kill. We also adjusted the period for moose hunting in order to avoid the calving season.

BLANCHE WEST (TULK)—MY SISTER

Earlier that year, 1998, on March 20, I lost my only sibling—my older sister, Blanche—to cancer at the age of sixty-two. It broke my heart, and there is still a searing, burning emptiness in my chest.

As a politician you need to have a thick skin. You can't let anything thrown at you wipe the smile from your face. I could, and can, deal with all that. But matters of the heart are different. You don't shrug them off, nor should you. Blanche not only died too young, but she never realized the true potential of her talents.

She did get to have a family, whom she loved dearly.

She was way smarter than me, as I said earlier, but left school in grade eight to get married. She never got back to furthering her education. She could write poems. She was a great seamstress—like our mother. I used to tease Mom, who made sixteen coats one winter, that if she didn't know how to do something, she should call Blanche.

Blanche was very competitive, and she loved "beatin' Beaton." She could have beaten me in anything, academically, and career-wise if she'd had the same breaks or luck that I've had. Her health declined as cancer got its grip on her, and I worked out of an office in Clarenville, where she was hospitalized, for the last few months of her life. That enabled me to visit her much more often. Sometimes those visits would be over the lunch hour.

I'd bring in some scratch tickets, we'd divide them equally, and we'd play them while we talked and ate. Even in her final days, weak and hardly able to stay awake, she made sure that she had all her tickets finished before I could get mine done. I love you, Blanche, and the loneliness haunts me still.

FIVE MONTHS OF HELL

It was a busy year for me, work-wise, and a tough one emotionally with the loss of my sister, and then into the picture stepped one John Woodrow. Woodrow had established a paralegal institute in St. John's, a private college to train paralegals. Later, his licence to operate the same was revoked by the Newfoundland government.

Subsequent to that revocation, he brought a lawsuit against the government for $90 million. On November 24, at his request, he met with Harold Porter, a lawyer with the Department of Justice. At that meeting he alleged that he had paid bribes to get the licence in the first place.

Mr. Porter told him that he should put the matter in the hands of the police. He then informed the deputy minister of Justice, Lynn Spracklin, who the following day, November 25, referred the matter to Colin Flynn, Director of Public Prosecutions. Flynn referred the matter to the RCMP. Then, suddenly, on November 27, Woodrow requested and was granted leave by the Newfoundland Supreme Court to drop his lawsuit.

Then, on December 2, I was contacted by a journalist who indicated that she had been approached by Mr. Woodrow, who had made various allegations against members of my staff. He was also indicating that I was involved. I advised the premier right away.

I told Mr. Tobin that there was only one thing to do, in my opinion. I would resign my positions with his government, and we should get the RCMP to do a full investigation. I also wanted the Commissioner for Members Interests, Bob Jenkins, to look at whether I or any member of my staff had contravened the Conflict of Interest Act.

Tobin was reluctant to accept my resignation, and it was two or three hours before he did so. As we were about to go into the House, I said to him, "Either you get up and announce it immediately, or I will."

He did make that announcement around ten minutes after 2:00 p.m.—that I was resigning from cabinet until my name was cleared, and that we were referring the matter to the RCMP for a complete investigation.

I then spoke with the press and told them that I had resigned. I stated categorically that there was absolutely nothing to the allegations. I said, "I came into the House with my integrity, and I plan to leave with it."

The next five months were not pleasant—not for me, my family, nor Dora's family. On top of that, there was an election called in February of 1999, and I had to run in that election under a cloud of suspicion due to the investigations we had initiated.

Kevin Tobin's take on the Woodrow affair

I did get a lot of respect in the House. The members opposite treated me with decency, and the issue was never raised again. Out on the hustings, the constituents supported me and I came through that election with the biggest majority that I ever had.

I can't say enough about how Brian Tobin treated me. Even though I had resigned as Government House Leader and minister of D2R2, he kept me right beside him, still in the same seat. He knew I was innocent, and I believe he was angry that we had to go through this—these unfounded allegations and the investigations—in order to clear my name.

The investigation dragged on, and when we won the election, I resumed my seat in the House of Assembly with no cabinet responsibilities until my name was cleared. On March 18, the RCMP reported that there had been no criminal wrongdoing. On April 27, the Commissioner of Members Interest also reported that the allegations were unfounded.

The same day, Tobin announced these findings in the House, and the next day the headline in the *Telegram* read, "There's No Beatin' Tulk." A couple of days later, one of the people in his office brought over the original with the headline and the story done up in a frame. That was a nice little touch—I still have it, too.

On April 28, I was back in cabinet as Government House Leader and minister of Development and Rural Renewal.

The change of our name as a province from Newfoundland to Newfoundland and Labrador started back in Joey's time. His government began using the longer name on official documents and stationery. In 1992 a resolution was passed in the House of Assembly to start a process that would lead to a permanent name change.

In 1999, during the Tobin years, another resolution was passed by the House of Assembly and subsequently sent to Ottawa. On December 6, 2001, the constitution was amended to rename our province. By now Tobin was gone and Grimes was premier, but the provincial government which "got it done" was Tobin's. Also, our postal designation was shortened from NFLD to NL to indicate Newfoundland and Labrador.

The intention was to be inclusive—to assure the people in Labrador that they were part of a province, and not *owned* by a province. Joey's original moves were more to "scare off" Quebec, which had historically claimed Labrador as its own and simply ignored the official border between Quebec and Labrador on its provincial maps.

I believe that most people are comfortable with the name now, even though it is a bit long and unwieldy. Older people, like me, still have difficulty remembering to use the full name.

7

Transitions

The election on February 9, 1999, returned thirty-two Liberal members to the House—down from thirty-seven in the last election. Still, it was a comfortable majority with a combined Opposition of only sixteen members—fourteen Progressive Conservative and two NDP. We were able to get through a great deal of legislation.

In my own contest in Bonavista North, I received just over seventy-five per cent of the vote, besting Jim Cooze 3,943 to 1,277. I certainly took it as a vote of confidence, as the electorate's faith in me.

JOBS AND GROWTH STRATEGY

Economic recovery following the cod moratorium was aided by the rise of the shellfish industry, primarily crab and shrimp. I don't dispute John Crosbie's decision to shut down the cod fishery on July 2, 1992. He did what had to be done. Amidst the anger and frustration that followed, who can forget his words? "I didn't take the fish from the god---- water!"

With the establishment of the REDBs, the development of their strategic plans, and the enthusiasm that was becoming evident, on September 27, 1999, Premier Tobin issued an invitation to the people of the province to take part in a process that would take our economic agenda to the next level.

He set up an ad hoc committee of cabinet comprised of Sandra Kelly, Julie Bettney, Roger Grimes, Ernie McLean, Paul Dicks, and Kevin Aylward. I had the pleasure of chairing this Ministerial Committee on Jobs and Growth.

There was tremendous interest—I'd never seen the like before in this province—for such a consultation. Initially we had planned thirteen public meetings across Newfoundland. They were scheduled to be completed in the third week of November 1999. Interest was so great, however, that an additional ten of these public sessions were added, with the final one held in Hopedale, Labrador, on February 7, 2000.

We also held a number of "round table" sectoral forums, each exploring the major opportunities in different sectors of the economy—manufacturing, fisheries, and forestry, for example. To the credit of the government, Premier Tobin in particular, they were taken seriously, unlike many so-called "consultations."

Overall, we received approximately 300 submissions from these meetings. On March 22, 2000, an interim report became a major part of the budget speech for 2000–2001, where government announced its major themes and priorities to advance jobs and growth.

In October 2000, Premier Tobin returned to federal politics, and in the ensuing Liberal leadership race, Roger Grimes won and became premier. He continued using Jobs and Growth in budgeting for the province and as a means of pursuing economic development. On March 20, 2001, as the minister for the new Department of Industry, Trade, and Rural Development (ITRD), I presented the final report of the Jobs and Growth Strategy.

It was used again by Premier Grimes as the basis of his budget for 2001–2002. It was made clear that the report was to be a "living document," a permanent agenda, which might be adapted and adjusted as circumstances dictated. Again, in the 2002–2003 budget, $46.6 million was allocated to this initiative. In his final budget of 2003–2004, Grimes relied on the renewal strategy for creating jobs and growth as his economic plan.

His budget speech stated, "Our focus in creating the right climate for growth is giving the business community the means to prosper—wherever they operate in the province, but especially in rural Newfoundland and Labrador. The robust economic performance that the province is enjoying is due in large part to the success of our 'renewal' strategy."

The strategy begun by Tobin and continued by Grimes was working. On November 5, 1999, as Minister of Development and Rural Renewal, I was able to make this statement: "There is confidence among our people that we have turned the corner, economically, and as our 'friends' in the *Globe and Mail* recently reported, the Rock is on a roll.

"We are creating more jobs than ever before. Our economic growth rate is leading the nation. Investment is up. Exports are growing. Out-migration is slowing."

Again, on August 10, 2001, when I was deputy premier and minister of Industry, Trade and Rural Development, I was able to announce, "Our July employment numbers have increased by 9,000 or 3.9 per cent compared with July 2000, and all regions of the province have recorded employment growth."

The same was true for the 2002–2003 and 2003–2004 budgets. We were moving in the right direction of a diversified economy, where all regions developed, driven by the Jobs and Growth Strategy—"from the bottom up."

When one looks at the first budget of Danny Williams in 2004–2005, there is a seismic shift in the approach to social and economic development. Early in that budget speech, the statement was made, "Leadership in business will come from the top." That spelled the end of the rural development movement and the Jobs and Growth agenda that we had practised as a Liberal government.

One can only wonder, if our strategy had continued, would we have spent our offshore oil revenues by increasing our public service by fifty per cent and by increasing wages exponentially and prematurely? If investing at all, in projects like Muskrat Falls, would we have done it simply to prove to Quebec that we could? Was that the right approach? I doubt it.

Our regions would have been stronger, demanded to be consulted, and been a better guide to economic development than the "top down" approach which was now in place.

One of the primary planks of the Jobs and Growth agenda was the development of strategic partnerships in co-operation with business, labour, and community in order to build economic and social successes. Under the premiership of Roger Grimes, other ministers and I had the privilege of visiting Iceland, Ireland, and the Netherlands with union, business, and community representatives,

The experience of seeing things from the various perspectives of these observers, and from the viewpoint of the other countries, was tremendous. I believed that we were on our way to building a provincial economy with very solid underpinnings—with all hands pulling on the chain in the same direction.

Deputy ministers (DMs) are the most powerful people in the bureaucracy and, as such, can make or break a minister. John Scott was my DM in D2R2 and also in ITRD, for a total of about five and a half years. I used to joke with him in the mornings, "Where are you going to try to lead me today, John?" His reply was always, "Wherever you want to go, Minister." He was a hard-working, dedicated guy, a great policy person who guided the Jobs and Growth Strategy. He was very helpful with the project, and I was lucky to have him.

CENTRES OF EXCELLENCE

Another facet in our Jobs and Growth Strategy was the attempt to establish "Centres of Excellence" in various communities across the province. Central to this concept was the increased effectiveness and efficiency of the new age of technology and communications. To emphasize the point, I used to say, "You could create a successful business even on the Funk Islands with these new tools available."

We set about creating these Centres of Excellence through decentralizing the public service. We would move Forestry and Environment to Corner Brook, a natural fit, and Grand Falls would be an Internet Technology (IT) Centre.

Initially, we moved the Medical Care Program (MCP)—the submission and payment of medical and dental claims—to Grand Falls, as claims were now all being done electronically. Using air services as the first building block for an Aerospace/Air Maintenance Centre of Excellence, forty-seven positions were centred at Gander. We also assisted the Canadian Helicopter Corporation (CHC) with construction of a composite plant and, with that, the establishment of some 150–200 jobs there.

Forgive me for going off on a tangent like this, but I've really got to say something here about a guy I first met during the construction of that CHC composite plant in Gander.

Robert "Bob" Gosse was vice-president of CHC and the right-hand man of Craig Dobbin, the owner. Previously he had been director of air services, which also included the water bomber fleet. He was now charged with the responsibility of getting this plant up and running.

Busy as he was, he took the time to advise me, put me in touch with the right people, and help in any way possible to further our goal of creating an Aerospace and Air Maintenance Centre of Excellence in Gander. After attending an aerospace/airline show and visiting the Sikorsky Helicopter plant in the US, it became quite evident how well-known he was in the industry and how well respected he was for his expertise.

Bob is still one of my closest friends. Through him I met a wonderful woman, Maude Gosse—his mother—and most of his family. This Mi'kmaq lady from the Port au Port Peninsula was a Benoit who married Bob's father, a Gosse. Together they raised nine children through the hardest of times and in one of the most difficult places to make a living.

Despite those handicaps, the children were all well-educated and successful. Several became millionaires. One is in the Order of Canada for the rescue of a drowning man. Another son became a canon in the Anglican Church, and yet another served Canada in the armed forces. Two of their four daughters became teachers, one an accountant, and the fourth one, who has a degree in criminology, works with her lawyer husband.

A finer, more successful family you would search long and far to find. I visit Maude, who is now in her nineties, as often as I can, and I am proud and humbled to say that my picture hangs on her wall right next to Joey's.

This is Bob's family, and like my own, they are very dear to my heart.

In the process of moving positions, and in some cases people, to create these Centres of Excellence, it is fair to say that all hell broke loose. As the minister responsible for moving people in the public services, I took most of the heat. We got push-back from the unions and from some of the people whose positions were relocated.

Much of the "heat" was generated by the fact that we moved too fast. You are always in a hurry to get things in place once an initiative is agreed upon.

Every government MHA and cabinet minister whose riding encompassed or touched upon these Centres of Excellence wanted in on the action. Understandably, as it would benefit their regions—although an election was not due for another three years. The idea was that the senior public servants would carry out this program in consultation with the Public Service Union.

Those employees who were upset felt so because of the rushed pace of the undertaking and the uncertainty which that brought. My good friend Tom Hanlon said it was a waste of the people's money.

The original idea was to move 278 positions to these new Centres—*positions*, not necessarily people. To minimize the disruption, we allowed people to transfer to lateral positions—positions that were vacant in other departments in St. John's—and for those who did move, we helped with house equity assistance programs.

Despite our best intentions, our best efforts, the storm that followed was rough. I was called Judas Iscariot and a number of other things you don't say in polite company. In the final analysis, we moved only forty to fifty people to fill 278 positions. I believe most of those people are now happy with the move. It also served to "spread the wealth" across the province as well as to establish those Centres of Excellence.

A few years ago, Dora and I were going to Florida, and we had to notify MCP that we were leaving the province for an extended period. I called the Grand Falls office, and the lady asked, "Are you the Beaton Tulk who is responsible for moving MCP to Grand Falls?" I admitted I was, and I expected a tongue-lashing.

"Well, sir," she said, "I want to thank you. I have never been happier with my lifestyle." For her, at least, it worked, and I hope it did for all the rest of those who relocated.

Decisions like that initiative won't always be instantly comfortable for those involved. In some cases I'm sure they'd never be. However, judgment requires that you have to do what is necessary for the greater good of many, disruptive as it may be to a few.

GOVERNMENT HOUSE LEADER

Some interesting things happened as well in my position as Government House Leader from 1996 to 2000. The main purpose of that position is to get legislation passed. You have to make sure there is ample debate, but the end game is the same: get it passed.

Thanks to my years in Opposition with people like Ed Roberts and Steve Neary, and as Opposition House Leader against such Government House Leaders as Gerry Ottenheimer and Bill Marshall, I came to know the rules of the House very well.

I loved the House, and I still do. There's a special feeling you get when you are in there—the feeling of responsibility. Whatever you do, or fail to do, it is bound to affect a lot of people. There's also something different about the people who congregate there. Underneath the heckling and the wisecracks, there is a feeling of camaraderie. I don't know if it's the same in other provincial legislatures, but in our House of Assembly there is an overwhelming sense of patriotism. No matter which side of the House you are on, when you meet outside, even years later, the feeling was still there—the feeling that you had done what *you believed* was right for Newfoundland, as had your opponent.

Of the hundreds of people I saw go through the House, I only met two whom I didn't like—only two I felt didn't belong there—but that is up to the people to decide. Oh, I was a heckler, too—not the worst, but certainly not a wallflower. I got back as good as what I gave many times.

One incident that occurred after the election of 1982 is a good case in point. All but a handful of us had been defeated in the Peckford sweep. We were an endangered species. I used to joke that we had bull's eyes on our backs and the only reason we didn't go down is that we were protected under the small game licence.

When the House opened, white-haired Steve Neary was our Opposition House Leader, and there were only seven more of us to back him up. For whatever reason, I started calling the government side "The Muppets." It was meant to imply, I suppose, that they were just a bunch of puppets—or yes-men—to Brian Peckford.

I called the Government House Leader, Bill Marshall, for whom I have great respect, "Kermit." I'd say things like, "Kermit is up again," when he'd rise to speak, and, "Kermit is instructing the other Muppets."

This went on for a few days until Len Simms, a minister in Peckford's government, looked across the floor one day and said, "I would rather be a Muppet than be in Opposition with Snow White and the Seven Dwarfs." He got me, and he got me good.

Of course it's not all levity, and sometimes the debate got very heated. The toughest time was during the nurses' strike in the Tobin years. The nurses' union and the Opposition put up a rambunctious campaign. The nurses had banners and bumper stickers that said, "We *Will* Remember, Mr. Tobin," or words to that effect. There was anger and many short tempers—on both sides.

Eventually, our government, the Liberals, brought in back-to-work legislation. The House was in bedlam for much of the debate, with people in the gallery shouting and others banging on the doors outside. Late at night, when the bill was passed, the premier, cabinet, and government members took an unorthodox way out of the building and escaped with our skins intact.

I learned of secret passageways in Confederation Building that I had not seen before. We got out, away from the crowd that was gathered out

Store# 00146 Coles Avalon Mall
48 Kenmount Road
St. John's,NL A1B 1W3
Phone: (709) 753-3394

YOUR FEEDBACK MATTERS.

Tell us about your visit for a chance to
win a $500 gift card. Complete our
survey at: www.indigofeedback.com. No
purchase necessary. See survey website
for Contest Rules.

Store# 00146 Term# 002 Trans# 777876
Operator: 570AH   09/10/2018 15:03

SALE
****
MAN OF MY WORD $19.95
9781771176705
****
Items : 1

Subtotal: $19.95
GST: 5.0% $1.00
Total: $20.95
CASH: $21.00
Change: $0.05
****
With our free plum rewards program,
you could have earned 100 plum points.
Join today!
****

Store# 00146 Term# 002 Trans# 777876
GST Registration # R897152666

0014600207778761

primes privilège^{MC}
plum™rewards

Points requis / Points Required	Valeur de la prime / Reward Value
2 500 / 2,500	5 $ / $5
4 500 / 4,500	10 $ / $10
8 500 / 8,500	20 $ / $20
20 000 / 20,000	50 $ / $50
35 000 / 35,000	100 $ / $100

Inscrivez-vous gratuitement! Visitez indigo.ca/primeprivilege.
Join today for free! Visit indigo.ca/plumrewards.

Chapters   Indigo   COLES   indigo.ca

primes privilège^{MC}
plum™rewards

Points requis / Points Required	Valeur de la prime / Reward Value
2 500 / 2,500	5 $ / $5
4 500 / 4,500	10 $ / $10
8 500 / 8,500	20 $ / $20

front, and went off somewhere together to try to gather ourselves and to process what had just happened.

THE SHOP CLOSING ACT

One of the longest debates we ever had was an Opposition filibuster over the Shop Closing Act. This was a piece of legislation that allowed stores and other businesses to open on Sunday. To a great many people, Sunday was a religious and family day.

The Opposition took the position that the government was destroying our moral and family values. We, as the Liberal government, were of the opinion, as liberals should be, that these values should not be legislated but should be left up to individual personal choice. If you don't want to take your family shopping, then you don't have to. If you want to take them to church, you can. If you want to have your whole family over for a big Sunday scoff and then fall asleep on the couch, more power to you. This act would not force anyone to do anything.

If, however, you want to go shopping, you should be able to—perhaps it's your only day off together. If shopowners wanted to stay open, that was their decision. The people and the market should decide, not the government.

So the battle was on. The Progressive Conservative Opposition under Ed Byrne, member for Kilbride, vowed that we would not get the legislation through. I vowed that with the number of members we had compared to them, even if we had to debate around the clock and wear them out using a shift system, we would get the bill passed.

After about forty hours of debate, and with the Opposition using every tactic and device they could think of to stop us, the bill was passed. Mr. Byrne once told me that he had looked at every tactic I had used as Opposition House Leader. I don't know why he didn't use the reasoned amendment approach. I was expecting it but was not about to tell him. My objective was to get the legislation through and move on to something else.

As Prime Minister Winston Churchill was quoted as saying, "No one pretends that democracy is perfect or all-wise. Indeed, it has been said that democracy is the worst form of government—except all those that have been tried from time to time."

Despite all the work and stress of trying to run a province—complicated by the huge size of its geography and its low population and all the infrastructure needs that these factors dictated—we had a premier and caucus who loved to get a laugh at each other's expense. In that regard, Premier Tobin was as good as any.

BEATIE'S PILLS

During the Cabot celebrations of 1997, I travelled from Twillingate to Greenspond on the *Matthew*. It was being towed by the Coast Guard ship *Groswater Bay*. My wife, Dora, who was then a supervisor with Aliant, decided to call the ship-to-shore operator in St. Anthony to give the captain of the *Groswater Bay* a message for me.

The message was: "Tell Beatie not to forget his pills." I took the message—wondering if there was an emergency at home—but so did half of Newfoundland and Labrador! Every ship, fishing boat, onshore support person, and anyone else with a radio scanner was following the *Matthew* and heard the message.

Wherever I went for quite a long time afterwards, people wanted to know if Beatie had taken his pills today. We had a night sitting on one occasion where Kentucky Fried Chicken was the meal. We were sitting around the caucus table, eating supper and planning our evening back in the House, when Dora arrived with my medication.

Immediately, Premier Tobin began ragging me. "Here comes Dora with Beatie's pills." Everyone had a laugh and joined in the teasing.

Not satisfied with that, the premier said, "You know, b'ys and girls, Dora even puts on Beatie's socks in the morning." That was followed by another round of laughter. Then he made a tactical error by not letting it go.

"And which foot do you put on first, Dora?" Brian asked.

Without a moment's hesitation, my darling wife looked him straight in the eye and replied, "Premier, whichever foot might *rise to the occasion* and present itself to me." Tobin had been had this time, and the last laugh was Dora's.

PASSING THE BATON

The winds were changing again, and in the spring of 2000 it became apparent that Premier Tobin might be about to make another big move. Dora and I were in Florida, and we were invited to Craig Dobbin's place to watch an eclipse of the moon. George Furey—who later became a senator and Speaker of the Senate and was then one of Mr. Tobin's prime political advisers—was there.

There was obviously something already afoot. When we went in to Dobbin's apartment, I was greeted by George Furey as "Deputy Premier." I asked, "What are you talking about?" He just laughed. Then, later in August 2000, while I was waiting for Mr. Tobin to come out to a meeting regarding the Centres of Excellence, Tobin's secretary came out and said, "You have to go and see the premier in his office."

I got up from the table, went into his office, and already there were Art Reid, an ex-minister, and Gerry Glavine, who had been his chief of staff. When I walked in through the door, Brian said, "Deputy Premier, Gerry is going over to the Liquor Control Board, and Art is going to be my new chief of staff." I nodded.

Tobin asked, "Did you hear me just call you Deputy Premier?"

I looked at him and replied, "Any raise?"

"Not likely," he said with a laugh, and then I sat down.

There was some turmoil in Tobin's personal life at the time. His father was dying of cancer. Brian's wife, Jodean, being a nurse, wanted to bring his dad home, where he would be more comfortable and get more personal care—and Brian wanted to spend more time with him. Whether that was the reason he appointed me at that time, I don't know, but I did assume some of his duties going forward, including running his office, when he was not there.

At the time, there was about to be a federal election. There was no secret that the federal Liberals would have some problems in Atlantic

Canada. Tobin, with his strong national profile—"Captain Canada"—would be invaluable in holding seats and turning some others to the Liberals. I'm sure that Jean Chrétien thought so, too, and the rumour had been going around for some time that he wanted Tobin back in Ottawa.

The rumour grew stronger after I was appointed deputy premier, as it looked like he was clearing a path to leave. I believed that he would be good for Newfoundland as a federal cabinet minister—and if by going back he might have a shot at prime minister when Chrétien retired, it would give us a prime minister from this province and as a result get the attention we sorely needed in Ottawa.

He was to be appointed to cabinet and then seek a seat in the upcoming election. I know that he was offered Foreign Affairs, which is high-profile, but I told him he should go for minister of Industry. I told him, "There's not many votes for the leadership of the party in any foreign country." Little did I know that the infamous date of 9/11 was just around the corner. That catastrophe, bad as it was, would have certainly raised his profile internationally. It would have given him a high platform from which to be heard. In any event, he accepted the Industry portfolio.

We had a caucus meeting, and Brian announced his intention of running federally. It all happened so fast, I don't remember if we even had a vote, but the caucus agreed with him that I should take over his position as premier—until a leadership convention could be held. One of the conditions was that I would not seek the leadership at this convention. That was fine with me, as I had no desire to seek the leadership.

So, on October 16, upon Mr. Tobin's resignation, I was sworn in as premier of Newfoundland and Labrador. If I had wanted the leadership job, I would have run for it at that time. After I *had* the job as interim leader and took over the premier's office, I realized it was the best job in Newfoundland and Labrador.

I openly stated that the premier's office would not be supporting anyone in the upcoming convention, and I personally picked no one either. I stayed neutral. On the second or third day in office, Jim Thoms from NTV asked me if I would come down and do an hour-long interview with him. I agreed.

I noticed when I walked on the set that there was an extra chair besides the ones Jim and I would use. We had just sat down and were talking when in walked Geoff Sterling—owner of NTV—and he started asking questions of the new premier. It went very well, and I felt good about my performance.

Then I started getting calls and messages from all over the province—and elsewhere. The common theme was, "Where has this guy been hidden, and why is he not running for the leadership of the party?" There were a number of people who contacted me and said they wanted to put forward a "Draft Beaton Tulk" petition.

However, I had made my decision, so whether or not I had changed my mind was a moot point. The biggest single thing against me, had I run at that time, would have been that I was now using the office of premier to become the elected leader and permanent premier. So, I didn't run. The interview and the resultant buzz from it certainly helped my self-confidence as I performed my duties over the next few months.

WILDCAT STRIKE

I had probably done just about everything in the House—in either Opposition or in government—over the years. The one area with which I was unfamiliar was Treasury Board. Treasury Board was responsible for negotiating union contracts.

A few days into my new job, Anna Thistle, who was president of the Treasury Board, told me that a union lady representing the lab and X-ray technicians was coming in the next day to talk about negotiations. Their contract had expired, and she wanted to get new negotiations started. I said to Anna, "I'm not familiar with that file. Would you ask her if I could have a couple of days to get familiar with it?"

Unbeknownst to me, this woman had made several attempts to get a meeting. It had always been put off, for whatever reason, and perhaps the reasons were legitimate. I don't know. In any event, she'd simply had enough "runaround." So, the next morning, I found myself in the middle of a wildcat strike.

Because it was a wildcat, and not a regular strike, I did everything I could to break it. I recognized the right of unions to strike in an unsolved labour dispute, but this was not the case here. I even threatened to get—and tried to bring in—people from the armed forces. If necessary, I would have dropped them down through the top of the Health Sciences Centre to get it done.

We had to open the House and bring in legislation to get them back.

In my five months, we got a good few things done. I gave the people of the Labrador coast—the Inuit and Innu—the right to ban alcohol from their communities. I had two great people, my clerk, Gary Norris, and my assistant clerk, Andy Noseworthy. These two dedicated and hard-working guys deserve much of the credit for what we accomplished.

On December 12, 2000, we announced a celebration for September 2001, "Receiving the World," to coincide with the one hundredth anniversary of Marconi's first transatlantic wireless message from Cabot Tower on Signal Hill. It was a convention designed to showcase the advancement of information technology in Newfoundland and elsewhere. It was a tremendous success.

On the same date, we also announced funding that would double the number of students attending the Marine Institute. Training for ships' officers, engineers, and crewmen was vitally important, I believed, to rural Newfoundland, and it was an important part of our strategy for Rural Development.

When I became premier, I had to give up the job of Government House Leader, and I had to appoint someone to take that position. I knew who I wanted. One of Newfoundland's great orators and a fountain of knowledge on parliamentary procedure is a man by the name of Tom Lush. I asked my secretary to get him on the phone. I figured he was around St. John's somewhere. However, he was in Halifax, Nova Scotia.

I passed a few pleasantries with him on the phone, and then I said, "I'm going to appoint you as Government House Leader, if you'll accept it. Now, I need to get you sworn in as a minister with the lieutenant-governor. How soon can you be here?" Tom had been left out of cabinet positions, somewhat unjustly, in my opinion, and was vegetating on the backbenches when he had so much more to offer.

"Brother, my front wheels are already in the water, heading back across the gulf," he replied. I don't know whether he flew, took the ferry, or skimmed over the waves in his car, but he was back in St. John's the next day and was sworn in as Government House Leader.

We also put in place a review of the Freedom of Information Act and were able to complete quite a number of other things. At the end of the five months, Gary Norris came to me and said, "You know, you got quite a bit of work done in a short time." I believe we did.

THE LIBERAL LEADERSHIP CONVENTION

The convention was held in St. John's on February 3, 2001. Running were Roger Grimes, John Efford, and Paul Dicks. It was a divisive campaign and convention. On the first ballot the results were: Grimes 609, Efford 546, and Dicks 111. The lowest one has to drop out before the next ballot, so the final choice was between Efford and Grimes, and the result was incredibly close: Grimes 638, Efford 624.

I spoke at the convention before the vote, and at the close of it, in an effort to try to bring everyone together. I'm not sure that it did much good.

The problem, in my opinion, was that the final vote was so close—fourteen votes out of some 1,262 cast was the difference between first and second place.

MY TIME WORKING WITH PREMIER GRIMES

On February 13, ten days later, Roger Grimes was sworn in as premier. Having had some time to consider his options, he quickly put together his cabinet. I was offered to stay on as deputy premier and to assume the ministry of Industry, Trade and Rural Development. Premier Grimes had combined the mandates of the former Department of Development and Rural Renewal and the Department of Industry, Trade and Technology into one. Even though it meant a great deal more work, I felt grateful to him for his confidence in me. For me it was another dream come true.

I believe that Roger said on the night of the convention that the first one he wanted to talk to was me. Next would be Efford and Dicks, who had run against him—because he wanted us all in his cabinet.

It was evident in the next few days that the rancour from the convention was still there. I tried to smooth over what was becoming an open split. On this particular night, before Roger was going to meet with John Efford, it was evident that there would likely be a parting of the ways between them. We didn't need that, and neither did the province. Both men were very talented and had been great Liberals all their lives.

I called Art Reid, who was the chief of staff for the premier, and told him that I needed to meet Roger before his meeting with John. We met at 8:00 p.m., and he was given the following proposition: that he would relieve me of the ITRD ministry, I would stay on as deputy premier and work on some of the large files—like Voisey's Bay and Churchill Falls—and that he would give John Efford the Industry, Trade and Rural Development portfolio. He agreed.

The premier met John and offered him the position. The events of the day bore that out.

The House was in session that day, so as we were going into the House, I said to Roger, "I must go over and speak to my old buddy." John and I were good friends. We'd travelled the province together and worked together on a few files. John seemed to be okay with everything. He wanted to know what I would be doing when an election was called. "You'll run federally, won't you? You've done everything else here," he told me. I told him that I really didn't know—and it was true at the time.

After the House closed that day, Premier Grimes called caucus together. At the start of the meeting, Roger stated that he had offered to make John the ITRD minister, but partway through that discussion he received a note from him saying that he couldn't accept. So, the attempt to heal the wounds was made, but it was not to be.

The Department of Industry, Trade and Rural Development stayed with me. Premier Grimes continued to support the Jobs and Growth Strategy in his budgets. Creation of the new department was a brilliant idea on the part of the premier. While all government departments are vital to the social and economic well-being of the province, most of the levers of economic development were under one roof.

It cannot be denied that large-scale developments such as oil and gas, hydro, mining, wind power, and solar are all very important. If developed right, they can contribute much to the economic, social, and cultural status of rural Newfoundland and Labrador. Without that type of attitude, the unique culture that we have historically developed in Newfoundland and Labrador will disappear. We will lose our character as a people and be no more. The governments of Tobin and Grimes recognized these two interrelated components of development. When Premier Grimes combined the two departments, one of my duties was the negotiation of industrial benefits for large-scale developments.

WHITE ROSE AND MARYSTOWN SHIPYARD

The first project was industrial benefits for the White Rose offshore oil development. We were adamant that whatever work could be done in Newfoundland would be carried out right here. We had received somewhere around sixty per cent of the Terra Nova development benefits. We wanted more for White Rose.

I well remember the first negotiation meeting. Present were the CEO for Husky Oil, their negotiator, Premier Grimes, me, and the Energy minister, Lloyd Matthews. He was firmly on side and was a great partner throughout the process. The premier opened the meeting. In his remarks, he informed the group that I would carry the negotiations for the government. After the others had made a statement, I was invited to lay out the government's position.

Rumours and rumblings were already out that the project engineering was to be done outside Newfoundland. I believed they were accurate. So, I started my remarks with a series of questions for the chief negotiator. I knew he had been here long enough to know the answers.

First question: "How do you regard the quality of our living accommodations and housing here?"

The first answer was very positive, indicating they were as good as anywhere.

Second question: "How do you regard our education system?"

The second answer was positive.

Third question: "Is there any problem getting in and out of Newfoundland through the airport?"

His answer, what I expected, was that except for weather sometimes, it was good and caused few problems.

At this point the gentleman was becoming a little perturbed and wondered aloud why I was taking this line of questioning.

Next question: "Why, given your answers, do you propose to do the project engineering outside this province? If you need to bring your supervising engineers here, I understand, although I do believe the skills can be found here. However, the engineering can be done here, as well as other project components that will be done here."

I wanted to be clear that was our goal and that would be our negotiating stance. When asked, the premier and minister of Energy agreed that was our stance and I spoke for the government. My deputy minister, John Scott, knew where we stood and, as always, carried out our expectations in an excellent fashion.

And so the negotiations proceeded to the point where we had reached eighty per cent of the project development, other than the construction of the floating hull, which could not be built here. Husky's position indicated that if they had to do more, the construction schedule would be compromised. Because of conversations held with some of their officials, we believed they could do a little more. Negotiations stalled.

On this particular day the premier, the minister of Energy, other political colleagues, and I were at an annual event in Corner Brook: the Premier's Golf Tournament. Now, I am not an avid golf player. As a matter of fact, I dislike golf and only played when it was necessary and expected. I could never figure out what was so great about pounding a little ball over green grass. So, what happened next was a blessing in disguise. Just before I was ready to go, the negotiator for Husky called to tell me that he was due to go in front of his board of directors that morning. He would have to advise them there was no deal on White Rose in spite of the fact that they had offered eighty per cent and that was all they could do. He wanted to tell me this might mean the loss of the project.

After a little back and forth, he asked me what it would take to get a deal. I replied that I had been told, by some of his own people—and I would not reveal who they were—they could do eighty-four per cent.

He asked me would I be available all day, God bless him. Given the importance of the project for Newfoundland, I would have been available in any case. But now I did not have to play golf either!

I was later called and informed they would do the eighty-four per cent, to which I replied, "You have a deal."

He wanted to know how he could be sure that I had that authority. I asked him if in the negotiations he had ever had reason to believe he had been misled, to which he replied, "No."

"So," I replied, "we have a deal, right?"

We had a deal, with all the benefits we believed we could get and still make the deal commercially viable. The premier and Minister Matthews were called to be told we had achieved what we knew to be the maximum benefits.

Concurrent with the negotiations on White Rose was the bankruptcy of Friede Goldman in Gulfport, Mississippi, in April 2001. The resulting effect on Marystown was devastating. Not only had the community lost its largest employer, but the shipyard itself was now the property of the company. The assets of the shipyard had been transferred from the government to Friede Goldman in January 1998. As such, it was widely believed the bankruptcy meant it could be sold by Friede Goldman for scrap.

As the minister responsible for the shipyard, I was questioned in the House of Assembly as to the government's intentions and accused of inaction by the Opposition. Fortunately, under the leadership of Wayne Butler, the Local 20 of the Marine Workers Union in Marystown were willing to work with their MHA, Minister Judy Foote, MHA Mary Hodder, and government to rescue the yard. One day when the Opposition came at me to be honest and admit that we had no control of the situation because the shipyard was being controlled by interests in the US, I made the assertion we would not allow "one wrench" to be moved—a promise I was not exactly sure we could carry through.

We tried on many occasions to get Friede Goldman to come to the province and discuss the issue. All to no avail. The best we could get were half-hearted commitments via telephone that the company hoped to protect the assets from a bankruptcy sale. Not good enough, was the feeling of all concerned parties.

So, it was decided that Minister Judy Foote, Mary Hodder, Deputy Minister John Scott, Wayne Butler, President of Local 20, two of his fellow union directors, the director of Industrial Benefits, and I would meet with the company in Gulfport, Mississippi. We wanted to ensure that all sectors were given the opportunity to tell the company how serious we regarded the situation.

Mr. Scott arranged the meeting and a chartered aircraft to take us to Gulfport after determining that it would be cheaper than the use of a commercial flight, given the fact that we could leave one day and arrive back home late the next day. It cost approximately $23,000 for all seven people. Of course, the media figured that was an awful expense.

Anyway, we arrived in Gulfport, and the next morning we met with the officials of Friede Goldman and their legal people. We had decided that everyone would have their say. It was agreed that, as the minister responsible for Marystown Shipyard, I would lead negotiations.

After we got in the heat of discussions, the deputy minister, Mr. Scott, asked if we could break for coffee. It was quite unusual for Mr. Scott to take a break. We did, and I asked him why. Referring to their negotiator, he said, "I know him, and he has a tendency to get hot under the collar."

"Oh," says I, "he does?"

After coffee we returned to the table, and I decided to test the negotiator's mettle. He soon learned we would not be scared by such antics.

The next step was to hold up an article from one of the local papers describing the direst of circumstances for Marystown Shipyard. I suspected that some of it might be coming from the company itself. This suspicion could have been right or wrong, but in any case, using the prop,

I sent the message loud and clear that neither the Marystown people or government needed the headlines, and we would do everything in government's power to ensure not a wrench was moved out of Marystown Shipyard. Again, a bold statement, but not as harsh as it was about to get.

We had a couple of aces up our sleeve. The negotiator for Friede Goldman was probably aware of them as well but wondering if we would use them and how. We played them in Gulfport, Mississippi.

When the provincial government sold the Marystown Shipyard to Friede Goldman in 1998, the agreement required the company to meet employment targets for 1998, 1999, and 2000. Friede Goldman had not met these targets for 1999 and 2000. Therefore, it owed a debt of $10,000,000 to the provincial government.

Secondly, we knew that Husky, in agreeing to maximize the industrial and employment benefits to Newfoundland from the development of White Rose, believed the Marystown Shipyard was vital to realizing that goal. Government knew that it would not end up owning the Marystown Shipyard but that it had a great opportunity to see it purchased by another private company.

As the lead negotiator, I put three options forward for Friede Goldman's consideration, with a three-week deadline: Lease the shipyard to a reputable company for a nominal amount of one dollar; sell it for what it had cost them to another private company; or the government would move to expropriate, if necessary through legislation.

Friede Goldman's negotiator had minimal trouble with the first two options, but he retorted that I would not dare to undertake expropriation, as it would portray Newfoundland as a "banana republic." My reply was, "You know that you owe us $10,000,000 for non-performance in Marystown, and while you are under Chapter 11 bankruptcy protection, any action we take would probably lead to the loss of that protection. Watch me and see what I would do."

The meeting finished, and we headed home. John Scott seemed happy, which made me believe we had scored and maybe won the game.

In any case, Peter Kiewit made a final deal with Friede Goldman for the purchase of Marystown Shipyard on March 27, 2002. The next day,

March 28, Premier Grimes and Husky announced the sanction of the White Rose project in St. John's. Meanwhile, Frank Smith of Peter Kiewit, Minister Judy Foote, MHA Mary Hodder, Wayne Butler, and I were in Marystown announcing the purchase of the shipyard by Kiewit. A great day for Marystown, the people of the Burin Peninsula, and Newfoundland and Labrador.

I still smile when I remember Wayne Butler's reminder to the press that without the "$23,000 charter to Mississippi" we would not have been here announcing a $2.35 million project. Strange, but his comment never got reported.

While with Premier Grimes, we announced other projects, such as a new adjustment strategy for the dairy industry, the Marconi celebration, the first cultural trade mission in Newfoundland and Labrador's history, and the strategic partnership initiative between labour, business, and government.

Then I started down the federal election road, which led to my political demise.

Premier Grimes continued to do great work. His signing of the Voisey's deal in June 2002 has provided employment and opportunity that will endure for years to come. Unlike many of the deals that have been done in this province, this was fully debated in the House of Assembly. The Opposition Leader, who allowed you could "drive a truck through the loopholes in the deal," did not bother to change the loopholes when he became Premier Williams just a year later. Instead, the truck-and-loophole analogy would have been more appropriately applied to his "signature deal" called Muskrat Falls. "Boondoggle" is better.

GHOST OF THE UPPER CHURCHILL

Before ending this piece, I have to talk about a matter that haunted my twenty-three years in politics, namely the Upper Churchill deal.

That the Upper Churchill deal has been a tragedy for the province is beyond a doubt. In terms of construction, its cost to the province was practically nothing.

However, from what I can gather, at least some of the problems in that contract came about as a result of the Churchill Falls (Labrador) Corporation beginning construction on the project before the deal was finalized. A letter of intent had been signed in 1996, and a finalized contract in 1999. That was three years after construction had begun. In the letter of intent there was no "escalator" clause whereby CFLco would benefit from any price increases in the market price of electricity.

Final contract negotiations dragged on.

It is worthy of note that the president of Hydro-Québec was a director on the CFLco board of directors. Very convenient for Hydro-Québec!

Three years into construction, with no finalized contract, CFLco found itself financially strapped, and Hydro-Québec was making demands which were not contained in the letter of intent. Renewal of the contract would no longer be by mutual consent and take into account increases in price. Rather, Quebec demanded a contract extension of twenty-five years at $2 per MWH, bringing the life of the contract to sixty-five years and with no escalator clause.

Studies have shown that if we were getting a "just" proportion of the revenues from the sale of the generated power, we would have been a "have" province for years. In addition to that, successive governments have spent millions, and indeed hundreds of millions, in negotiations and legal costs trying to reverse the course of events. But it has been to no avail. In essence, we have been told repeatedly, "A deal is a deal," and, "A contract is a contract."

As citizens of Newfoundland and Labrador, we feel that the deal in large part has become embedded in our political culture and soul. We have seen attempt after attempt by successive governments to negotiate a deal on the Lower Churchill and/or Muskrat Falls, only to fall short and have the negotiations become a political football by awakening the ghost of the Upper Churchill in the minds of the electorate.

As a point of interest, it is worth noting that the government was not involved in these negotiations. They were conducted between the Churchill Falls (Labrador) Corporation, the British Newfoundland Development Corporation (BRINCO), and Hydro-Québec. There is some indication that when CFLco officials called Joey Smallwood to tell him a contract was finalized, they neglected to tell him about the changes made to the letter of intent.

Be that as it may, the Upper Churchill deal was a tragedy for Newfoundland and Labrador. My concern is and always has been that it has become a cause of political paralysis whenever there is an attempt by government, particularly Liberal, to do any sort of deal with Quebec on power development All you have to do, politically and without justification, is push the idea that this is another Churchill Falls deal, and the public gets up in arms.

I have been asking myself for years why we don't just learn the lessons contained in that deal. What's done is done, and let's make sure that when 2041 comes and the contract expires twenty-three years from now, we get a just return or pull the switch and move on. With lessons learned, why do we not just move on to do other projects and judge them purely on their own merits? To do otherwise is fruitless, unless we believe that we are not as good as Quebec at the negotiating table. I don't believe that to be the case.

The last or second-last effort was by Premier Grimes in 2002. I say second-last because I am told that Premier Danny Williams attempted to get a deal, at the beginning of his government, with Premier Jean Charest of Quebec. His deal was conditional on the Quebec premier opening up the Upper Churchill contract. Of course Charest said no, as I suspect Danny would have said if the shoe were on the other foot. Charest knew it would mean political suicide in his own province. Although I was no longer in government at the time, it is my understanding from former premier Roger Grimes that a deal was close. In August 2002, an agreement in principle was reached between Premier Grimes and the premier of Quebec for development of the Lower Churchill (Gull Island). According to Premier Grimes, it was to be debated in public before finalized. What happened?

The ghost of the Upper Churchill rose again from the Leader of the Opposition, who labelled it another giveaway by a Liberal government. Knowing Roger Grimes, I cannot see that scaring him off. He brought the

Voisey's Bay project to the legislature, debated it, and got approval. Why did he not bring this one or, if there were problems, go back to the table?

Discussion on the deal seems to have ended in December 2002. Premier Grimes tells me that at one point the Energy minister threatened to resign. However, I believe it was probably a matter of timing. Keep in mind that you have to win elections to continue your agenda, and 2003 was an election year. If you were going to have a battle with this project, then the risk of not getting it finalized and approved before an election was too great. Given the feelings in our souls about the Upper Churchill—the "ghost"—God knows what would have happened.

Personally, I have always liked Danny Williams. Whether it is partisan or not, I have never been impressed by him as a leader or premier. Early on when I observed him in Opposition, it became obvious that his style of leadership was "my way or the highway" and "because I say it has to be done, it has to be done." That style of leadership often leads people to give you advice based on what you want to hear rather than what you should hear. I am told that as a hockey player Danny was very competitive, and if you did something to him, he would have to get you back. It is the only reason I can think of for his decision to desert development of the Lower Churchill and develop Muskrat Falls, with less than half the energy of the latter. Having failed like everyone before to get an agreement with Premier Charest of Quebec, he had to score a goal and win the game.

Maybe he believed that if he got a deal similar to the one proposed by Grimes, he himself would be haunted by the ghost of the Upper Churchill and lose a great deal of his popularity. In my own mind I have discarded that notion, because his popularity was so high, and being a Progressive Conservative as opposed to Liberal almost ensured that he could have survived a fair deal with Quebec for development of the Lower Churchill. I find it difficult to believe that Danny Williams intentionally sat down and knowingly put together a deal that would bring the type of cost overruns and rate increases for electricity that a great many people now suspect will occur.

Another theory is the belief that Newfoundland and Labrador is awash in oil and, given the price of oil at the time, we would pay for

Muskrat Falls out of our royalties. However, oil is a commodity, and like all commodities, its price rises and falls in the market. Even if it stayed at a high price, are we still not using money that could be used for more urgent needs? Did we really need this power at such a price?

However, after talking to a great many people about this whole tragedy, I can settle on nothing other than the "pure ego" theory and the thought that without the "ghost" we could have averted what now appears to be the "boondoggle legacy" of Premier Danny Williams.

THE ATTEMPT TO GO FEDERAL

I stayed for a year with Roger in the roles he had assigned me, and I had no qualms about it—until John Chrétien decided he wanted me to run federally. When Tobin went off to Ottawa, George Baker was the federal minister in charge of the Atlantic Canada Opportunities Agency (ACOA).

George got appointed to the Senate, thereby leaving a vacant cabinet position for Tobin—there was normally only one Newfoundland cabinet minister. Tobin ran in Bonavista–Trinity–Conception, won, and got his cabinet position, but that still left George Baker's old riding—Gander–Grand Falls—without a member.

In January or February of my last year, I went on a trade mission in place of Premier Grimes to Russia and Germany, along with some feds including Chrétien, and the other provincial leaders.

I had been avoiding Jean, as I felt, somehow, that he had kept Brian Tobin away from seeking the leadership of the federal Liberals. That was a very disappointing turn of events for me and many Newfoundlanders. I had heard that Chrétien was going to ask me to run federally, so I was ignoring him. Although we had been good friends, I was "browned off," you might say.

I was sitting in the plane one day, and when I looked up, there he was, leaning over me and beginning to speak. We chatted for a few minutes, and then he said, "I am soon to be calling that by-election, and you will run for me, no?"

"I'm not sure, Mr. Prime Minister," I replied.

Even though I was happy working with Premier Grimes, with my job and everything else, when the prime minister asks you to run—when you get the opportunity to participate at the federal level and help your province (and I believe I would have gone directly into the cabinet)—you run. So, I did. I lost.

The by-election was called, along with six others across the country, for May 13, 2002. I had a high profile in the province, I was well-known locally, and it should have been a sure bet. This is meant in no way to denigrate my opponent, but he was young, new, and inexperienced. Everyone seemed to think this would be a shoo-in for me.

I had a gut feeling early on in the campaign that it was not going to be easy this time. I had that feeling once before, in 1989, when I was defeated by Sam Winsor in Fogo. I couldn't convince my team that we needed to do even more and work even harder. They were so sure that we would win, that it was impossible for me to lose, but the result showed that it wasn't just nerves.

I make no excuses for losing. The people are always right, but there were a few reasons, I believe, for why I lost. It was a big, spread-out riding, not just the two main towns but numerous small communities included. We were not as well organized as we should have been.

I declared for the candidacy and ran unopposed. There may have been some political influence that kept me unopposed. I don't know that for a fact, but if it did happen, then no doubt there were some hurt feelings, some Liberal supporters disaffected. Only 19,210 of the 55,260 eligible voters (34.8 per cent) went out to vote. That is not exceptionally low by by-election standards. We lost by about 700 votes.

Also, at the time there was still some resentment against Brian Tobin for having left Newfoundland. He had been a very good premier, well-liked and respected, but there was a feeling that he had left to pursue his own agenda, that he sort of walked out on us. I compare it to a father leaving home. No matter what the circumstances, the children will resent it—some for a long time. Here was Tulk now, his right-hand man, about to do the same thing.

When I left to run in the by-election of May 13, I went out to my riding of Bonavista North. I promised the people there that there would be a strong candidate to replace me when the by-election or general election was called. We had someone in mind who would serve the district well.

After the federal election, that candidate backed out, so my old district was left with no strong Liberal candidate. A poll was done to see whether I would be acceptable as a candidate. The question was asked, "Do you care that he left to run federally, and now he wants to come back?" In other words, "Will you support him?"

The response was positive—somewhere in the high sixties percentage range. I knew in my gut that this would not hold until election day.

I went to Premier Grimes and told him that if he wanted me to run, I would. If he didn't, then I would not. I think he believed that I had the best chance of anyone to hold the district. The Liberal tide was receding. We all knew it. I ran, and I lost.

Danny Williams was already on the move. He had been elected leader of the PC Party. A multi-millionaire who knew how to run a number of companies should know how to run a small province, right? As I write this, I believe a similar sentiment, circulating in the USA, certainly helped elect Donald Trump as the forty-fifth president. Let the reader, and time, decide whether that was a logical assumption.

The mood for change was growing, though, and there was division in the Liberal Party after the close results between Roger Grimes and John Efford in the leadership convention. Some Liberals who supported the losing candidate were not so enthusiastic. You need unity and enthusiasm at the district level.

Perhaps it's just wishful thinking or cold comfort for me, but I think that had I stayed with Bonavista North instead of running federally, I might have held it for the Liberals. I might have eked out a win there and maybe helped a couple others of our members in close contests.

Brian Tobin announces Jobs and Growth Strategy, 1997

Left: Premier's Portrait in 2000
Right: Jean Chrétien and me on a Canada trade mission to Russia and Germany, 2001

Tobin, Chrétien, and me in Corner Brook during the federal election in 2000

Clarence Chaulk, his wife, Marilyn, and me
at my desk in the House of Assembly in 2000

Being sworn in as premier by Lieutenant-governor Arthur Maxwell House

My cabinet as premier

Thank You Minister Tulk
Sandstone Elementary
Ladle Cove, Nf
Education Week 2000

A visit to Ladle Cove Elementary in 2000

"Keep the meter runnin'"

Premier certification plaque

8

Canadian Transportation Agency

After my defeat in Bonavista North, I went from being totally immersed in my work as minister and deputy premier, twenty-four-seven, to being totally unemployed—really for the first time in my life. Usually people in politics spend more money than they make. I was no different. You borrow money to finance your campaign. Contributions are usually small, especially if the contributor thinks that your party will not win government.

If you win government, it is no better. When you get in, everyone expects something from you. Wherever you go in your district, someone is having a draw for something, someone is selling tickets, and someone is looking for a "small" contribution. I'm certainly not complaining, as it was a privilege to sit in the House of Assembly, either side.

You put up a prize for a contest. You buy someone a lunch. Your budget is only so big, so you dip into your own pocket. You pay your own expenses to go to many events which you are expected to attend.

As Jean Chrétien told me once in his own unique way, "If someone will be going into politics to become rich, they will not like the surprise they will have." To make a long story short, I needed to work. I couldn't sit back and wait until my pension kicked in—and I *wanted* to work.

THE CTA BOARD APPOINTMENT

Then, on December 16, 2002, I was appointed to the Canadian Transportation Agency (CTA) board by Prime Minister Jean Chrétien. While it was unexpected, I was not surprised.

Let me clarify that last statement. I had been a long-time supporter of Chrétien and his policies. We shared a common position on so many issues—poverty, indigenous affairs, growing the middle class, and so on. I had even left provincial politics, where I was comfortable, to run for him federally. He had promised me nothing, nor had I asked for anything when that campaign failed—so the appointment was unexpected.

I was not surprised, though, because I knew the kind of person he was. He placed a high value on loyalty. When he heard of something that he knew I could handle, he made it happen. I accepted the appointment.

The job entailed sitting on the decision-making board of CTA, to which complaints were referred for resolution—a quasi-judicial function in resolving air, rail, and marine transportation complaints. It was different from politics or my work in education, but that background sure gave me experience in making just, and I hope wise, decisions. I thoroughly enjoyed the work and met some great people—people like George Proud, Guy Delisle, Marion Robson (president), Gilles Dufault—who is recently deceased—and Geoff Haire, who replaced Marion when her term was up.

The CTA is an independent board—a tribunal and economic regulator. It makes decisions on a wide range of issues involving air, rail, and marine transportation under the Canadian Transportation Act and other related legislation.

In that position you can't make public statements on these or any issues, and you have to stay away from politics. I was sorely tested when a controversy arose "back home" about Dora's involvement in campaigning for me in my previous political life. Again, when comments were being made publicly by everyone and his brother during the "MHA expense scandal" back in Newfoundland, I was certainly tempted to speak up.

So, for the first time in my life, my political mouth had to remain shut. But politics gives you experience in legal matters and a rudimentary understanding of the law. Along with that, we were each given a number of training sessions when appointed to the board on how to conduct ourselves, on fairness and balance in the law, and on what it meant to be a member.

As a board we had to deal with complaints about issues in the air sector, on everything from airline tariffs, treatment on airlines, and international tariffs, to lost luggage. The rail sector regulating involved primarily central and western Canada—issues like cost of shipping grain, availability, and service. In the marine sector, most work involved ensuring that Canadian vessels which were available and suitable were used in Canadian waters.

I didn't move to Ottawa, although I liked the city, but remained in the Goulds. I spent about two weeks a month in Ottawa—when the board was meeting—and the rest of the time working from home. They set us up with a desk and a computer, and we were in constant communication. Two board members would have to sign off, for example, on any foreign-based charter coming into the country.

AIRLINE REGULATIONS

We had an economist and a legal team on staff. So, when a complaint came in we had the benefit of their knowledge and advice on a particular issue in terms of the legal and economic ramifications of any ruling we might consider.

We had to travel across the country in many cases to hold hearings and in some instances to see first-hand the true nature of the issue. In other cases we could work out of Ottawa and bring the complainants and the accused together to work out a solution or a compromise through mediation.

For example, at one point the Canadian airline industry would not allow a passenger to take their own oxygen aboard, even though they required it, medically. The airline industry insisted that you use its supply and apparatus. The argument, of course, was that its own was inspected regularly and that other supplies coming aboard might not be examined so stringently and thereby cause a safety hazard for all on board.

The complainant's position was that the airlines were charging too much for their oxygen and using this essential service—to those whose medical conditions required it—as a "profit centre," just another way to make money. The cost, for example if you were flying St. John's to Toronto, return, might be $600. The customers could supply their own at a fraction of that cost.

We ended up ruling that a customer could take his or her own— from a certified supplier.

Travellers with allergies was another national issue, as was equal accessibility for people with disabilities. These did not require site inspections but required a fair amount of travel—with hearings across the country. We'd hear from all the parties involved and then have to reach a fair decision.

While I was there we made rulings on all these issues—allergies, oxygen, and accessibility. The first two were relatively simple to resolve. The latter, accessibility for people with disabilities, was more complicated and had occupied the CTA for years.

That issue boiled down to: Should these persons travelling with an attendant or attendants pay one fare, or pay for their attendants' fares as well as their own? In their "tariff," the airlines had already defined disabled persons who might require an attendant, i.e. type and severity, and they made the decision as to who qualified.

At issue, then, was: Who should pay for the attendant's/attendants' seat/s required? The airlines' position was that every seat taken must be paid for. They had been unwilling to change, as they felt anything else would be open to abuse and so become unreasonably costly.

We assembled a panel to hold hearings. There were three of us at the start, but one member's term expired, so it was left to me and Gilles Dufault to make the final decision. The hearings took many weeks across the country. We heard from disabled individuals, groups for the disabled, the individual airlines, and others.

The airlines, in particular, indicated that any deviation from their position would require a huge increase in fares to cover the cost. The airlines were well represented in these hearings. They had lawyers and consultants aplenty. We spent many hours in our deliberations with our own lawyers and economic staff.

To me the decision was simple—it came down to the rights of disabled people as Canadians, and what it would cost the travelling public, at large, by way of increased fares. Our economist had done the research and the math, and he indicated that the additional cost per ticket would fall in the range of $0.75 to $1.50.

I looked across the table at our economist and said, "So, you're telling me it would be the cost of a small, perhaps not even good-quality cup of coffee?"

"You could put it that way," he replied.

Using my political experience, I made the argument that I believed no Canadian would accept less than equal access for disabled persons, given so low a premium. One of the consultants for the airline industry raised the subject of abuse again. He argued that the public would take advantage of it, everyone would want an attendant, and it would cost the airlines a fortune—and so on and on. Finally, I interrupted him.

"Do you realize something?"

"What should I realize?" he wanted to know.

"Do you realize that the airline industry has *already* decided who qualifies, who needs an attendant? It's in your tariff. What the Canadian Association for the Disabled is asking is that once *you've* determined that an attendant is required, that you provide the extra seat for the attendant at no cost to the disabled person."

"Oh, is that so?" he asked. "We already have the right to determine who needs one?"

"Yes, you do," I told him.

So, the theory that this minor accommodation to the disabled would bankrupt the industry flew out the window. I had been in public life for thirty-some years, from a backbench Opposition MHA to premier of a province, and if I ever made a decision of which I am proud, that was it.

RAILWAYS

My experience with trains was confined largely to a few trips I had to take from Gander and Gambo to St. John's and back when I was attending Memorial University. As soon as I could afford to buy a car, that experience was over.

Trains in Newfoundland are long gone now, so it's easy to forget how important they still are to central and western Canada—to the mining, shipping, and agricultural industries in particular—and how vitally important they were, historically, as a nation-building device. I learned a lot about these things with the Canadian Transportation Agency.

As a board we took two trips through the Rockies and into the prairie provinces. Both Canadian National and Canadian Pacific took us through, as a way to show us what they were up against in terms of scheduling, weather, and other factors in order to provide this service.

We switched trains partway through the Rockies and often had to pull over to a siding to allow other trains to pass. About thirty-five trains a day were passing through this line. Imagine that: thirty-five trains, 120 cars long, many of them with containers stacked two high on flatbeds. I was amazed by how much product was being shipped from Asia into west coast ports and then overland by rail to market.

It was indeed an eye-opener for me. We had briefing sessions all day long on the challenges presented by this line. I, for one, could not help but marvel at the obstacles human beings had overcome to make those railroads a reality. The narrow mountain passes, the bridges, trestles, and tunnels defy imagination.

The cost in terms of human life and money it took to lay out the route, to blast through mountains, and build across canyons in order to link the country together gives you a sense of pride and humility at the same time. Sir John A. Macdonald's determination was certainly great, and his vision, once realized, certainly justified it.

I stared in awe at places like the Devil's Gorge, where we went on a rail a hundred feet in the air and looked down 120 feet or so at rapids between two mountains. In another place the rail had to go up over the mountain, and since you can't have a grade of more than two per cent, you wound *through* it, slowly, and when you finally came out at the top, you could look down and see the last few cars—the tail end of this 120-car train—just entering the tunnel below.

Where John A. Macdonald, as a politician, got the courage to attempt to build such a magnificent structure at the time, with the tools that were available then, is a question someone else will have to answer. In my mind he stands as tall as any peak we saw. Today, with all our knowledge and technology, I wonder if we would say, "We can't afford to do this."

Would Macdonald listen to Danny Dumaresque's idea of creating a permanent link, via tunnel, for Newfoundland under the Strait of Belle Isle? I think he would. Rather than be subject to the vagaries of the weather in the Gulf, the commercial traffic both to and from the island portion of Newfoundland and Labrador would be facilitated. More importantly, the linking of Newfoundland to Quebec would facilitate tourism between these provinces.

Most important, though, is that it would serve to bind the country together. Any isolated area—anywhere—turns to introspection and sees only its own problems and challenges. This, a mindset in Newfoundland for a long time, has only moderated a little since Confederation. Would British Columbia have become or remained a part of Canada without the links? Who knows? Build the tunnel!

MEDIATION

Mediation was taking on a much more important role in resolving disputes during my time at the CTA. I enjoyed that aspect more than any. When you can get two opposing sides together around a table, magic can happen.

More often than not, the two parties share a common goal. Once they discover that and agree to work out their differences in approach, it is indeed fascinating to see what can happen. You see the change in their eyes, their mannerisms, and their body language. When you start seeing smiles and handshakes as they come together in a "team" to achieve the common goal, it is very rewarding.

While I was working on a mediation between CP Rail and a resort owner in Alberta, I arrived at the town late in the evening only to discover that I had no luggage. For my meeting, at eight o'clock the next morning, I had naught but the clothes on my back—my travelling clothes: an old T-shirt and a pair of jeans. Thank God the Walmart was open.

There were no other places to get clothes at that time of night, and if you know me, you know I am ample in size. In any event, there was very little choice at Walmart for a tall, heavyset man.

I managed to find a pair of pants (too long in the leg) and a brightly coloured Hawaiian-style shirt like you might have worn on a cruise—in the 1960s—and tried to make the best of it.

The next morning at the start of the meeting, my travelling companion, another guy working with CTA, looked at my turned-up cuffs and said in front of all, "You got shorter last night, did you?" Everybody laughed. I know I must have looked ridiculous.

It was, however, a great icebreaker—exactly what you need to warm up a meeting. After a brief discussion, we went to the site to inspect it.

The problem was the resort owner had built his lodge up on the hill above the railroad tracks, and on the lower side of the tracks—at water's edge—he had a "nature preserve" for the enjoyment of his guests. He wanted a railway crossing there so the guests could drive from one site to the other. Unfortunately, it was down a steep hill and therefore too dangerous for a crossing. Reducing the grade would have been a very expensive proposition requiring a lot of blasting. We walked the whole area in order to understand both sides of the dispute.

Within three hours, though, we had a solution and an agreement. The solution was for CN to build a longer road from the resort to a more level area and put the crossing there. Mediation worked to the satisfaction of both parties.

Another instance involved CN Rail and Lantic Sugar, a processing company in Montreal. The rail company was using one of its engines to shunt carloads of unprocessed sugar to Lantic's refining plant once every two or three hours because Lantic's facility could only accommodate three cars at a time.

The rail company's position was that it could no longer afford to do that—as it was, they were tying up an engine and an engineer all day long, for just a few minutes' work every three hours. Lantic filed a lack of service complaint. I was asked to go and mediate.

We had the first meeting in Toronto, and we got nowhere. It was too difficult to visualize the problem without seeing the site. Both parties agreed to go to Montreal to have a look. Two weeks later we met again, in Montreal, and began by touring the site.

We discovered that the railroad company had an unused rail there—a spur on which they could store a number of cars of sugar. The company agreed to allow Lantic to use it and to help Lantic purchase their own shunter so that they could retrieve these loads themselves at their own convenience. The rail company's engineer suggested this, and it would work for all. We almost had the deal done.

But then the Lantic plant manager wanted to get in his two cents' worth. He felt he had to go on the record as saying that the rail people were "oppressors." There were lawyers, engineers, and the top management of both parties at the table. I didn't want to lose the deal. I could see the rail lawyer's face change—he was ready to call off the deal.

I rolled my wheeled chair around from the end of the table and moved in next to the plant manager. With my arm around him, I said, "You look like an oppressed man."

Everyone burst into laughter, including his boss, who spoke up quickly with, "Beaton has this problem solved for us. It's over."

I had no authority as a mediator to impose a solution. If mediation—a mutual agreement—did not work, then Lantic would have had to go back to the CTA and a solution would have been imposed. It's so much better when you can help two parties reach their own agreement rather than impose a compromise that keeps no one happy. And we got this one done without my having to dress up funny.

So, as I said earlier, I enjoyed mediation, and I believe I came to be very good at it. If I were younger, I would have launched another career in this field when my time at the CTA was up.

After my five and a half years there at CTA, I retired. I was to miss this rewarding work and the ability to visit often with my three children, who lived in Ottawa and are still there.

9

The Tulk in Winter

I'm not so sure I like my title for this chapter. Now in my early seventies, I like to think that I am in no more than the late autumn of my life. Despite my age and having done pretty well everything I wanted to do—with very few regrets—I would still like to live a lot longer.

Retired now, I have time to visit Dora's family and mine—time to enjoy my grandchildren and one great-grandchild. As you approach the "winter" of your life, you tend to look back more than you look forward. You think about all the valued long-term relationships you've developed and those people you looked up to and from whom you learned.

I've already talked about some of the most important people, the ones I love: Dora, my children, my parents, my sister, Blanche, and the rest of my family. I've talked about people who inspired me in education, in business, and in the civil service—people like Lloyd Dennis, Bob Gosse, Clarence Chaulk, and others. But I'd like to say more about some of those I worked with in politics.

I hope none of what you read here is "actionable," as my lawyer would say.

I should say that the nickname "The Incredible Tulk," which at one time Laurie Blackwood Pike and I considered as the title of this memoir, originated from *Telegram* cartoonist Kevin Tobin, who drew me as a superhero of sorts in his daily comic. That editorial cartoon appears below. I don't consider myself incredible in any sense of the word, but it is a nice play on words, and I decided to show it off.

Beware "The Incredible Tulk," 1982

THE PEOPLE OF THE STRAITS SHORE, GANDER BAY, AND FOGO ISLAND

Before talking about politicians, I want to thank all the people of this area who elected me from 1979 to 2002—in the beginning as their MHA for the district of Fogo, and later as their member for Bonavista North. The one exception was 1989–1993. The person to blame for that loss is, in large measure, me.

I could almost name them all, but that would take another book, and worst of all, I might omit a name or two of those who voted for me or helped me in some other way.

I speak of those who gave me donations which they often could ill afford, and who campaigned with me, door to door, in all kinds of weather, those who invited me into their homes for a snack and apologized that what they had to offer was not good enough, those who defended me when I was wrongfully accused and celebrated with me when I was vindicated, those who trusted and believed in me, and carried me on their shoulders, even when I lost.

For the first ten years they put up with me being in Opposition, knowing full well that the chances of a Liberal government were practically zero. Not once was it ever suggested to me that I should cross the floor—this despite the political atmosphere at the time, which meant they would get very little in the way of services with me in Opposition. They asked only that I speak up for them and try to help.

They also gave me the opportunity to meet and work with some of Newfoundland and Labrador's and Canada's leaders in my political and other careers. For their loyalty, I will be forever grateful. These are *my* people, and they are more important to me than I can adequately express.

LEO BARRY

I said earlier that Leo Barry had been a good leader and how difficult it was for me to take part in his removal when the time came to do so. If he had succeeded in winning the election and become premier, I believe he would have governed well.

JEAN CHRÉTIEN

It is difficult to think about him or write his name without a smile coming to my face. The self-styled little guy from Shawinigan with the twisted grin and the broken syntax found his place in the hearts of Canadians from coast to coast. He considered himself a common man, an ordinary man, no different from the rest of us.

One night in 2000, after a rally in the Corner Brook area, he invited Brian Tobin, me, and our wives to dine with him, his wife, Aline, and their daughter France. We talked about a number of things, but I'll always remember what he said about Canada.

"Here we are, Brian—you and Beaton and me. You were premier for Newfoundland, and now you are minister of Industry for Canada. Beaton, he is the premier for Newfoundland and Labrador, and me, I am the prime minister of Canada. Our fathers, they have worked hard. Your father a fireman, Beaton's a lumberjack, and me? My father, he worked in a factory in Shawinigan.

"Because they worked hard, and this country is called Canada—the greatest country in the world—their children will be able to succeed. Why will anyone want to destroy a country like this?"

Campaigning in Stephenville in October 2000 with Prime Minister Jean Chrétien

Chrétien did not get his job easily. He ran against John Turner for the leadership of the federal Liberal Party in 1984. Because of a modern "tradition" of alternating between francophone and anglophone leaders, many felt, after Trudeau—who himself in reality was half French and half English—being a francophone, that it was an anglophone's turn. Turner won, immediately called an election, and lost in a landslide to the Progressive Conservatives' Brian Mulroney.

Within a year or so there was a move for a leadership review in view of that election loss. Chrétien supporters were allegedly behind it. Many people considered Turner to be "yesterday's man," who had only won the leadership because he was an anglophone. I got a call from Turner to meet for lunch in Ottawa.

We met, and he asked me in a diplomatic way if I was part of the movement. My answer was no, as I believed it would not be good for the Liberal Party, or Chrétien, as it would cause a split in the party. I also believed that he, Turner, deserved another "shot at it." Turner lost that next election, picking up only a few more seats.

In the next leadership race and convention in June 1990, Chrétien won the hearts and minds of his party and defeated his nearest rival, Paul Martin, Jr., by 1,500 votes. Jean went on to become one of Canada's finest prime ministers. I'd call him a pragmatic intellectual—but not the least bit aloof, as intellectuals tend to be—and very capable of using grit and charm to solve problems.

The people of Canada obviously agreed with him, as he was elected three times as prime minister. In my opinion, he could have won a fourth term.

He was happiest and most comfortable with ordinary, common people. I remember in 1984 he took a tour of the Fogo district with me. It was the dead of winter, and he landed on the airstrip, as excited as a kid going to the carnival. This was Friday, and he was scheduled to speak the next day at the provincial Liberal convention in Gander. The weatherman was calling for a dreaded nor'easter on Saturday. However, we had committed to a dinner and dance, so it had to be done.

We had a big crowd for the dinner at the Fogo Island Central High School, and the dance was being held across the road, at the Fogo Island Motel. It was said at the time that this motel had the biggest dance floor east of Montreal. Off in one corner, the b'ys were playing darts. When we arrived, I took him in there first.

He watched for a bit and then said to one of the boys, "I suppose the biggest score will be if you hit the bull's eye, no?"

"Oh, no, Mr. Chrétien," buddy replied, "it's the triple twenty." Jean stepped to the line, threw one dart, and it lodged firmly in the triple twenty. Now, that's how you get your "street cred" from a group of dart players! It may have been pure luck, or he might have been a good dart player. We never found out.

Someone asked, "Do you want to play a game?"

"No," he replied, "because if I will beat you, then you may not vote for Beaton." I heard him tell the story several times, later, at affairs which I attended.

The following day, the helicopter arrived without incident, and we went on to my home community of Ladle Cove. At the town hall we met a number of people from my childhood, and we had our picture taken with my son, Conrad. From there we were off to Aspen Cove, where David Tulk made him the honorary fire chief of the fire department.

Next we went over to Clarence Chaulk's "Southfork," where Jean met with the national news media. We also visited Lumsden, Musgrave Harbour, and other communities in my district. That night in his speech at the convention in Gander, he told the dart story. It was a weekend I won't soon forget.

A few years ago there was a picture in the news of Chrétien waterskiing on one ski. He was holding the tow line with one hand and waving to the crowd with the other. He was then eighty-one years old. Methinks the triple twenty was not pure luck. Jean came up the hard way. He certainly could handle himself, as he demonstrated on a protester with the "Shawinigan Handshake" and when he put the moves on a burglar at 24 Sussex.

Today I count Jean Chrétien as a friend. He remembered me after I suffered two defeats in one year, and perhaps he felt somehow responsible. I don't know. In any event, when he appointed me to the CTA in December of 2002, I did my best to be worthy of the position, and I believe that I was.

JOE GHIZ

I first met Joe at an Atlantic Liberal leaders' meeting. Joe was then Liberal leader in PEI, and I was president of the Liberal Party of Newfoundland and Labrador. Also present there were Sandy Cameron, Nova Scotia's leader; Ray Frenette, interim New Brunswick leader; and Steve Neary, Newfoundland and Labrador's interim leader. I was there at Steve's invitation.

We had no Liberal governments in Atlantic Canada at the time, and the meeting had been arranged to find ways and means to revive our fortunes.

Joe had lost the previous election to the PCs but had won his seat. However, two years after our meeting, he won the election and became the Liberal premier of Prince Edward Island. I found Joe to be super-intelligent, charismatic, and simply quite charming. Here was a man destined to achieve whatever he set his mind to do. His election as premier came as no surprise to me. A great orator like Joe Ghiz, in the style of our Joey Smallwood, Don Jamieson, and Brian Tobin, was bound to move the electorate in his direction.

Several years later, as personal friend of Premier Clyde Wells, he was invited to speak at our Liberal convention at the Holiday Inn, St. John's.

He held the audience spellbound. I'd been late getting to the convention from Fogo Island, so my group had to stand back by the door in this packed room.

As the room rose and cheered at the end of his speech, I lost sight of him in the crowd and began talking with those who came with me. Then I heard a voice saying, "How are you, Beaton?" It was Joe, standing next to me, and we chatted for a few minutes.

Some of my crowd were anxious to get to my suite, where we could sit down after having to stand for so long, and because of our long journey into town. I explained this to Mr. Ghiz, and he said, "Do you mind if I come with you?"

"I'd be honoured," I said, and away we went.

Within ten minutes it was as if my constituents had known him all their lives. We were bantering back and forth and killing ourselves laughing. He sure had the common touch. Some considerable time later, a knock came on the door. Clyde Wells stood there. He was looking for his good friend and guest.

"Sorry, Clyde," said Joe, "I was having such a good time that I forgot to check my watch."

Joe's biggest accomplishment in government—he had many more outside—was the Confederation Bridge to PEI. It was a divisive issue, but he took a stand and is widely credited as the reason that PEI is now permanently connected to the mainland of Canada.

Jean Chrétien and me at Premier Joe Ghiz's funeral in PEI in 1996

After leaving politics he became Dean of Law at Dalhousie University in Halifax. Later he was appointed as a justice in the Supreme Court of Prince Edward Island. If he hadn't died of cancer at the young age of fifty-one, there's no telling what else he would have accomplished.

I was honoured to represent the Tobin government, along with Joe's good friend Clyde Wells, at his funeral. Joe Ghiz, one of the great ones.

ROGER GRIMES

I knew Roger and his Liberal family for years before he got into politics. Roger came out of the teaching profession, like me. He became a well-respected president of the Newfoundland and Labrador Teachers' Association. It was no surprise, then, when he ran and won the election as the MHA for the Exploits district.

I got to know him as a friend and a colleague in the House of Assembly. He soon became a senior cabinet minister in the Clyde Wells and, later, Brian Tobin administrations. A major player in the change to secular from the denominational system of education in Newfoundland, Roger was a straight shooter and tough as nails.

In the 2010 leadership convention, he won the leadership over John Efford by fourteen votes. It had been a difficult campaign, and unfortunately the closeness of the vote had a divisive effect on the party.

Roger replaced me as premier of Newfoundland and Labrador subsequent to that convention. To his credit, he didn't ask for my vote during the campaign for leadership, nor did he ever ask me afterward if I had voted for him. He respected the fact that I had announced at the start of it that the premier's office and I, personally, would stay neutral.

In setting up his cabinet, he combined the old D2R2 department with another to create the new Department of Industry, Trade and Rural Development (ITRD). He offered the ministry of this department, along with the deputy premier position, to me.

This was perfect for me, as it allowed me to continue the work I'd done under Premier Tobin with an even more extended range. I thoroughly enjoyed every moment of the work for a year, after which I offered federally in Gander–Grand Falls, and if that wasn't painful enough, I returned to Bonavista North to contest that seat for Roger.

It is clear, in my judgment, that Roger tried to heal the rift in our ranks after the rancorous leadership convention. I am sure that he would agree those efforts failed. The tide had changed in Newfoundland and Labrador, and the PCs under the populist leader Danny Williams were coming on like a tsunami. I don't fault Roger. That wave was unstoppable. Unfortunately, the next receding tide left a lot of flotsam and jetsam on our shores, of which the Muskrat Falls fiasco is a significant artifact.

At another time, Roger would have been re-elected and governed successfully.

DON JAMIESON

In 1979, the year of my first political campaign, Don Jamieson was convinced by the Liberals to return to Newfoundland to lead the provincial party in the election. I had gotten the party's nomination for the Fogo district while Bill Rowe, who had resigned, was still the leader here. Don was considered to be one of the best politicians, and indeed a statesman, both here and nationally. He was a legend in the Trudeau government.

Loved by his constituents—where he connected them to the rest of Newfoundland by road—he was greatly respected in the rest of the province. He was well-known from when he was a television news anchor on CJON as the man with the photographic memory and the silver tongue.

I remember when he landed in Gander, and the Liberal Party and the people from our district were invited to the rally. On that day, he could have been elected premier. He was a star, and the people loved him. As the campaign wore on, though, his silver tongue was silenced by laryngitis, and the PCs, under their new, youthful leader, Brian Peckford, started coming on strong.

We ended up with nineteen seats, an improvement over 1975, but were still in Opposition. Even serving in Opposition with Don Jamieson was a treat. He was a brilliant orator. When he rose to speak in the House, even the PCs and Premier Peckford were spellbound.

Few people ever left their seat when he began. He could go off on a tangent, have you hanging on to every word, and then dramatically, as easily as a writer inserts a comma, come back to his subject without missing a beat.

He loved being around people. He would often invite members of the caucus back to his place for a swalley and to chew the fat. He was very fond of Derrick Hancock, who got elected in a by-election in St. Mary's–The Capes. He went by the name "Dick," and he was very brash and outspoken. Don always called him Richard instead of Dick, but he loved it, and Jamieson would laugh like hell when Dick would call him something rude in place of Don.

The day of Don's retirement, we were all backstage waiting to wish him farewell and good luck. When Don arrived, Dick spoke up. "I'm going to miss you, you old f-----," and Don replied, in his proper and formal voice, "And I'm going to miss you too, Richard." He meant it. Don Jamieson, one of Newfoundland's great ones.

STEVE NEARY

After the 1982 election, Len Stirling resigned and Steve Neary became interim leader of the Liberal Party. Because no one else wanted it, I ran and was elected as the president of the party. As a result, Steve and I spent a lot of time together and became good friends.

Steve was the best in the province in getting under the skin of the premier and his ministers. He loved it so much that I almost think he would have liked to be alone in Opposition so he could do it more often.

He had been the member for Bell Island and a minister in the Smallwood era. Bell Islanders loved him, and he had a loyal following among the working class. He considered himself one of them. He coined the phrase "ragged-arsed artillery." If he saw any policy or proposal which would harm the working class, he was the first one on his feet to fight it.

My father loved him, and although he never admitted it, I was sure that he voted for him in every leadership convention where Steve was on the ballot.

In the House, he was fearless and did not hesitate to bring to light any corruption or wrongdoing that he saw.

Ministers feared when he rose to speak, and he forced some of them to tender their resignations. If government members left when he was speaking, he would get his Opposition members to leave and then call for a quorum. You needed fourteen members present for a quorum. If there were not enough, the Speaker would have to adjourn the sitting, and of course the government would be embarrassed.

In would rush the PC members, like puppets on a string. If they did not stay, he would repeat the call.

Steve always believed that those of the "uppity" class in the Liberal Party opposed his leadership. He was probably right.

He was not opposed to taking a smaller-calibre shot at one of his friends, either. After his retirement he attended Dalhousie Law School, but he was back in St. John's before Christmas, in the House, and sitting in the Speaker's Gallery. I saw him there and went over to speak to him. Of course he knew that I was the Opposition House Leader. After our initial greetings, he looked around the room and then, turning to me, said, "And what *genius* is running this place for the Opposition now?"

He also stayed a very close friend of Joey Smallwood up until the day he died. Steve visited him regularly, right up to the end, and he was probably the best friend Joey had at that time in his life.

Steve died at too young an age from heart failure, and Newfoundland lost one of its great parliamentarians. His wife, Mary, requested that I be a pallbearer. I was proud to do so. Good old Steve. May he rest in peace.

Edward Roberts being sworn in as lieutenant-governor. L-R: Tom Rideout, Beaton Tulk, Premier Roger Grimes, Edward Roberts, Clyde Wells, and Brian Tobin.

EDWARD ROBERTS

Ed Roberts was the best and most intelligent premier that we *never* had, in my estimation. In terms of analyzing legislation and being able to project the likely reaction to, and consequences of, said legislation, he had no equal. Certainly in regards to his greatest strength, which was his frankness to the point of being abrupt in saying what he thought, he was a cut above all others. Some saw it as a weakness.

If you were to ask who influenced me most in terms of learning how parliament functions, my answer would be Ed Roberts. He had a biting tongue that made opponents leery of coming up against him. They knew they were going to get back worse than they gave.

Planting my Premier's Tree at Government House
with Lieutenant-governor Edward Roberts in 2003

Many did not want him to be the leader of the Liberal Party. Some found him arrogant. Although he and I had a few spats, I never took it as arrogance. I took his reactions as coming from a guy with a very sharp wit cutting to the chase rather than dilly-dallying around.

I remember clearly one incident early in my first term in the House. We were in a caucus meeting, and Ed came into the room and said, "Getting elected is not important. Getting *re-elected* is the trick."

When I got re-elected he said, "Now, Tulk, getting re-elected is not the goal. It's getting re-elected as many times as I have." I think, at the time, he'd been re-elected five or six times. I just looked at him and said, "But I didn't get elected on Joey Smallwood's coattails." He wasn't pleased by my analysis of his success, and of course he was right. Ed was always elected on his own strengths and abilities.

As lieutenant-governor, Ed Roberts was the first to really open up Government House to the public. He saw it as a public institution, and he carried the office of the Queen's Representative in Newfoundland in the best manner of any of our lieutenant-governors. The truth of the matter is, I regard him as one of the best people that I have ever met, and I count him as a true friend.

JOSEPH ROBERTS SMALLWOOD

The most influential person in my approach to politics, from my childhood on through my career in education, was none other than Joey. He was a hero to every outport Newfoundlander—including those of my family. Joey Smallwood did more for Newfoundland than any other person who ever occupied the top office in our province—before or since Confederation. There can be no doubt about that.

He opened up the place where I came from, and a multitude of other communities, to the outside world. He gave us some of the basic comforts that those in other places took for granted. People used to make fun of him as "the family allowance guy." For a lot of people who had nothing, and I mean *nothing*, that family allowance bought groceries for the kids and put clothing on their backs.

Joey was *particularly* the person who advanced education in our province more than anybody else. He built bigger schools, as frugally as possible, by having a standard model that could be replicated in multiple locations.

When they opened, you could leave your little one- or two-room school and, with the help of a bursary, go to one of these and get your grades nine to eleven and so be ready for university or trade school. I would never have gotten to Memorial University without one of these schools.

Joey built highways. There are numerous places in the province similar to Joey's Hill in Ladle Cove—places where he cut the ribbon or gave a speech when the road went through: those roads put through in order to open up communities to the modern world.

Sure, like his detractors claim, he tried to build industries in Newfoundland and a number of them failed. The point, though, is that he *tried*, where none had really tried before, and it was always about Newfoundlanders. He was accused by his opponents of being a rogue and a thief. I don't believe a word of it.

His own comfort was the last thing on his mind. Edward Roberts, who used to be his executive assistant, told me that when Joey went for a trip to China, he was about to leave with just the clothes on his back. Ed had to make sure he had suitable clothing wherever he went. Joey focused on his work—what he wanted to get done—and his appearance and comfort were the least of his concerns. That's who Joey was.

He started Newfoundland and Labrador on the road to where we are today. When he retired after twenty-three years as premier, our debt was only $800 million—after all of the infrastructure and other investments and improvements he made. Today our current deficit is around $2 billion, and our total debt is probably close to $20 billion. So, how much money did Joey waste, compared to what some others have done?

The biggest thing Smallwood was pilloried for was Churchill Falls. However, Churchill Falls did not cost the province a cent. It was built by private enterprise. The lack of an escalator clause, of course, was the big mistake.

At the time, with the price of a barrel of oil at about $2.50 a barrel, who could have predicted where it would go? Oil, of course, governs the price of energy. Most experts would have predicted stability or a slow retreat in the price, given the increased availability and new methods of recovery. Also, who could have predicted the steep upward curve in the world economy and subsequent demand for oil?

Without a doubt, toward the end of his time, he became arrogant. No doubt that is why some of the people turned against him and voted against him in 1971. I voted against him, against his government, but only once. If he didn't like you, he'd call you "Mr." Every time he saw me after that, the conversation went as follows.

"How are you, Mr. Tulk?"

"Fine, sir," I'd say.

"Do you pray?"

"Yes, sir."

"Do you pray often?"

"Yes, sir."

"You should, too, after what you did. Do you think the Lord will ever forgive you?"

This went on for a long time, and finally, one day when we went through this routine, I tried a different tack. When he asked me did I think the Good Lord would ever forgive me, I replied with, "Yes, Mr. Smallwood, I believe He will, but more importantly, will you?"

Joey smiled and said, "You're learning, you're learning. You're not there yet, but you're learning."

I always respected him, as you might glean from my comments about him. Later, I grew to like him. I went to visit him once with Steve Neary, and Joey said, "How are you today, Beaton?" The "Mr." was gone, and he never asked me those old questions again. I think I was forgiven.

Joey was the best premier of the province. Yes, he made mistakes, and yes, Churchill Falls was probably the most costly one—although I believe Muskrat Falls, today, is a much bigger one. While I admired premiers Wells and Tobin, I think they, too, would agree that Joey was the best.

LEN STIRLING

Len and I were both elected the same year—1979—he in Bonavista North, and me in Fogo. We shared an office in Opposition that was about eight feet by ten feet—the very lap of luxury. After Don Jamieson retired, Len ran and won the Liberal leadership. Jim Hodder, MHA for Port au Port, and I helped run his campaign for leader. Jim became the Opposition House Leader, and I became party whip.

After winning the leadership, Len worked like a Trojan by scouring the province from one end to the other to try to put an organization in place. I travelled much of it with him and learned a lot of organizational skills from him. However, in the upcoming election, victory was not to be had.

Brian Peckford was at the top of his game, and the Liberals were reduced to only eight seats. It's all about timing, in politics, and in other times I believe Len Stirling could have won the election and become premier.

BRIAN TOBIN

I first met Brian Tobin when he was executive assistant to Don Jamieson. He was a buzzsaw. My first political event with him was during a by-election in Burin–Burgeo–La Poile, where we campaigned for John Nolan in the communities of Burgeo and Ramea. John lost the election by thirty-four votes, but we won Burgeo and Ramea. We never let anyone forget it, either!

I think it was the night that we got back from Ramea. There were three of us in the Gillett's Motel room in Burgeo: Brian, me, and John Dustan from St. John's, who was travelling with us. It had been a long day, we were tired, and Brian, still wired from the day of campaigning, decided to engage in a bit of horseplay.

Meanwhile, John sat nice and dignified, smoking a cigar in his big armchair. I don't know how it started—I might have been the instigator— but Brian said something to me like, "Look at you, you big overgrown bugger." I said something back, and the wrestling match was on.

Brian kept coming at me, full tilt, bound and determined that he was going to knock me over. Most times I was able to block him, due in part, no doubt, to my size. But as soon as I'd look away, he was coming again.

John, standing to the side now to keep out of the line of scrimmage, and just as dignified as ever, kept saying, "Gentlemen, you are *wrecking* the place," as he took another puff on his cigar. This went on for some time, and after a while the bed was bottom-up on the floor.

Eventually we calmed down, of course, and there was no real damage to the hotel room—just disarray. I don't know if Brian would even remember this event, as he was in his early twenties at the time. I mention it simply to show that he was an ordinary guy, not opposed to a bit of fun at the end of a long day's work.

A few months after that by-election, young Tobin appeared at my office door and asked me what I thought of his chances of winning the federal district of Humber–Port au Port–St. Barbe—in an election scheduled for February 18, 1980. I told him, "If you think you are old enough to be considered a man, you *might* win."

"Don't worry," he told me, "I will."

Brian was then twenty-six, but he looked eighteen, and win it he did. How wrong I was to even doubt it! He took to politics and people like a duck to water. I helped him wherever I could. He had charm, charisma, enthusiasm, and the ability to synthesize facts in order to make decisions like no one else I've ever worked with in politics.

He also jump-started my political career again when he became premier. I knew I wasn't going to go anywhere with Wells, and I expected Wells would be around for a long time. Brian gave me the opportunity to do what I entered politics for, in June of 1979—to be able to do things for my district, for working people in the province at large.

I admired the guy—as a person and as a boss. When he gave me Forestry and Agrifoods and made me the House Leader, that was a great start. When he moved me to the department of D2R2, he gave me everything that I ever wanted to be in government.

Some people might say that Brian Tobin used me. Of course he did. That was his job. I was his minister. But he gave me the freedom to do whatever I believed was best. As he said, "I'm giving you a lot of latitude, here. If you do something that raises the profile of the government in a good fashion, you know who gets the credit. If you mess up, you know who gets the criticism." That was fine with me.

I believe that he may have gotten that little gem from Jean Chrétien, back when Tobin had the *Estai* arrested on the high seas. Chrétien told him, "If it works, you will be a hero. If it fails, you will be a loser." Tobin won that one—and we still have a turbot fishery.

Tobin's idea for a big rally a couple days before the last Quebec Referendum on independence was another gamble he won. He had people brought in by bus, train, plane, and students by school bus to get that huge crowd. It was the enthusiasm generated by that rally, I believe, that tilted the scales on a vote that we were about to lose. Canada won, and "Captain Canada" had taken another considered gamble and won.

Because of his flair and his charisma, perhaps, there are those who say that Brian Tobin is a mile wide and an inch deep. I found him to be something different. Since he's gotten out of politics, he is now one of the VPs of the Bank of Montreal. You don't get there if you can't read people, if you can't make wise decisions.

I've also heard it said that he was overly ambitious. What's wrong with ambition? People with little ambition usually achieve little. He had an innate ability to handle people, and that, in my opinion, is why he was successful.

Because of Brian, I got to do what I always wanted to do in government—be a minister and make a difference in some people's lives. If it was because of his ambition that I was named deputy premier and, later, became Newfoundland's seventh premier, then that's fine with me.

Brian had a great work ethic, and he also had a sense of humour. I wouldn't embarrass him for the world, but I have to tell one more story about him. When I was Agriculture minister and he was premier, we went to the Strawberry Festival in Deer Lake. It's one of your duties, as a politician, to attend these events. Having the premier attend is sure to attract a bigger crowd, too.

Whether the crowd wants to praise him or bury him, he needs to show up and show support. Of course, with Tobin, he was welcome anywhere except perhaps at a PC caucus meeting. The day went well, and we were exhausted by the time we got on the government plane to go back to town. Someone might have spiked one of those strawberry shortcakes we had, too. I don't know, but I was a bit giddy at the end of the day.

We started discussing various issues on the way back, and one of those issues was the unfairness of the Upper Churchill hydro contract.

I said, "Mr. Tobin, do you know how we should blow this issue up—get some real attention on the matter? I should go down to Churchill Falls, on your behalf, and take twenty-five RNC officers with me. When we get there, they can guard the place—let no one in or out. I'll sit by the main switch, and we'll give the prime minister and the premier of Quebec forty-eight hours to reopen the contract, or I turn the switch off."

He turned to look at me, paused for a moment, and then said, "Not a bad idea, but why would you take the RNC?"

"Well," I said, "they are our police force, and in order to remove them, the prime minister would have to either send in the RCMP or the armed forces. That would blow the whole thing out of the water and become international news."

"It *might* work . . . it *might* work," he said, appearing to give it serious consideration.

Soon we were discussing another topic. We got in late that night, or early morning, and Dora picked me up at the airport. The next morning, about 8:00 a.m., the phone rang. I was still in bed—dead tired. I could see it was Brian calling, but I asked Dora to answer it. "Tell him I'm not here," I said.

"He's not here, Mr. Tobin," she told him. "He's on his way to Labrador."

"Oh my God! Oh my God!" I could hear him say. "How can I get a hold of him?"

"You might try the RNC," Dora told him. "He said he had to stop in there on the way."

"No, he's not! It can't be done! I've got to stop him!"

I couldn't let him go on any longer, so when Dora passed me the phone, I said, "What do you want this morning, Mr. Premier?"

"Oh my God," he said, "I thought you were gone! I was about to have a heart attack or a stroke—and about to fire you either way."

I'll never know whether he was seriously considering what I suggested on the plane or whether—much more likely—he thought *I* was serious and he was just trying to humour me. Brian Tobin, a wonderful premier and a good bit of fun to be around.

PIERRE ELLIOT TRUDEAU

I didn't meet him then, but I saw him for the first time in 1968. I was twenty-six and could not understand why younger people in their teens would scream and cheer when this older, balding man as much as looked in their direction. "Trudeaumania" was at its peak, and the youth of the country took to him like a rock star.

When the cheers died down enough for him to speak, he greeted the crowd, and pandemonium broke out again. This man owned the stage and the audience. It wasn't long after he began that I came to realize he was a different kind of politician.

He spoke of fairness and equality and of a "just society" being his vision of Canada. This was not your old-fashioned politician promising wider roads and deeper ditches or a chicken in every pot. This man spoke to your heart, your sense of right and wrong.

Fifty years later, his son—not the great orator his father was—speaks of the same kinder, more compassionate Canada. A startling contrast now to the mean-spirited right-wing policies of Stephen Harper. Here's hoping that Trudeau, Jr. can get us closer to where we were with Chrétien, and of course Justin's father, Pierre.

After his sweep to power in 1968, Pierre's great intellect, his coolness under pressure, and his courage were quickly evident. His determination to make us "masters in our own house" while remaining part of the Commonwealth, his quick response to the Front de libération du Québec (FLQ), and his disdain for the concept of an independent Quebec—tribalism—are nothing short of heroic.

He became the "philosopher king," and the respect he received on the world stage grew Canada's reputation as a modern liberal democracy. You couldn't be more proud of your country or your leader when he rose to speak.

The first time I actually met him was during my term as the president of the Liberal Party of Newfoundland and Labrador. I believe it was either winter or spring of 1982, at a Liberal convention in Ottawa. At the time there was a dispute between the federal government and Newfoundland's Peckford government over ownership and revenue-sharing of offshore oil resources.

While I didn't share Peckford's approach, there is no question that every MHA in our House of Assembly believed that Newfoundland should be the primary beneficiary—that the resource should be treated as if it were onshore.

On the flight to Ottawa, I began making notes for a letter to Mr. Trudeau on the issue, which I intended to send when I returned home. Upon arrival in Ottawa, the presidents of all the provincial and territorial Liberal parties were invited to 24 Sussex for a reception and informal meeting with Mr. Trudeau.

We were given a few minutes to speak, individually, with him and have pictures taken. Being the brash individual that I was at the time, I decided to speak to him on the offshore oil issue. I told him that he should sign a deal with Newfoundland on offshore ownership and benefits. I reminded him of his role in the Great Asbestos Strike of 1949, his belief in building just societies, of the founding of *Cité Libre* in order to change the economic, social, and political order in his home province.

I concluded with, "Undoubtedly you understand the desire by our province to use this resource to help shape our destiny as proud Canadians." I said that I would compose a letter to him urging him to sign a deal with Newfoundland.

I still have the picture taken that day—the one with the brash young man and the older, wiser Trudeau with a somewhat bemused but interested look on his face. It hangs on my office wall, and every time I look at it, I am reminded of what happened after I returned home.

Two weeks later, I received a letter from a woman in his office. I believe it was Heather Peterson. She said, "During your visit to 24 Sussex you advised the prime minister that you were going to send him a letter. He has requested me to see that he gets it."

I don't know why, but I never got around to writing it. I was kept busy with my roles in the House of Assembly and as president of the Liberal Party of Newfoundland and Labrador. Perhaps I thought it would have no influence. I really don't remember—but I wish I had written it.

In the fall of that year, while serving as Liberal Party president, I attended a national meeting of the Liberal Party of Canada. Iona Campagnolo, the federal president of our party, set it up for each of us to be introduced, individually, to Pierre.

"Prime Minister," she said, "this is Beaton Tulk from Newfoundland. Have you met?"

"Yes, we have met," he replied. "And by the way, Mr. Tulk, I have not seen your letter. Did you write it?"

I was certainly surprised that he would remember such a small thing, but knowing that Jean Chrétien and Newfoundland's Bill Marshall were holding discussions on the issue, I mumbled something like, "I think they will likely sign a deal, anyway."

At 24 Sussex Drive with Prime Minister Pierre Elliott Trudeau, 1982

With that bemused look on his face again, Trudeau said, "It is highly unlikely that Premier Peckford will sign a deal with me."

The next and final time that I met him was at the national Liberal Party board meeting just before the leadership convention in June 1994. He had just announced his resignation as leader and asked for a leadership convention to choose a successor.

As he exited the room later, he saw me sitting near the door and turned to say, "I guess I will never get that letter now, eh?"

"I guess not, Prime Minister," I replied.

"Have a good life," he said, and walked on.

I include this series of conversations with Mr. Trudeau not because I affected the results of the negotiations on offshore oil in any way, as I'm sure I did not. I include them as a tiny example of what his memory was like, of his great ability to catalogue and file away everything he read or heard and to retrieve it at will.

With all the important issues on his plate, with all the ministers, premiers, and Opposition leaders vying for his attention, with all the problems he worked to solve, how did he have the capacity to remember one little letter from one insignificant politician—a letter he hadn't even received?

That was Pierre Elliot Trudeau, Canada's best prime minister to date.

CLYDE WELLS

I had, and still have, a great deal of respect for Premier Clyde Wells. He was intelligent, principled, and had a great tenacity that was no more easily overcome than the grip of a pit bull's jaws on a soup bone.

In his time he was considered the poster child of the Liberal Party. There was great delight among the Liberals in general and, no less, I can assure you, in our entire caucus, when he decided to run for the leadership. I should say *almost* entire caucus, as I know there was one member who was not delighted. That member will remain unnamed here. It wasn't me, nor was it Winston Baker, his opponent in the leadership race.

In spite of the above, I had some fundamental differences with him about the political process. One was that he believed fairness and balance should be the order of the day. In reality, there was a problem with that in districts like Fogo, the district which I represented, and other districts which had been in Opposition for a number of years.

It was no secret that these districts in Opposition had suffered, unfairly, during seventeen years of Progressive Conservative government. My argument was that fairness and balance, as a concept, could only be achieved once these neglected areas received their fair share and had caught up with the others in roads, infrastructure, and schools—in essence, brought up to par with the favoured districts.

I knew that Premier Wells was principled enough to do what he said he would do—during his tenure as premier, he stopped the Atlantic Lottery Corporation (ALC) from advertising in any way, shape, or form in an effort to "protect" the people of the province—so we argued this point. I'm sure he did not change his mind, and neither did I. It is fair to say that Wells and I were like oil and water. While I admired and respected him—and I like him as a person—we could not mix, philosophically.

MAX SHORT

Max came from a small, isolated community on the Great Northern Peninsula called Lock's Cove. I've never been there, but by his description it was very much like Ladle Cove, where I grew up. Later, his family moved to St. Anthony. Lock's Cove is now a deserted place.

Max's family were all successful fishermen. He set his hand to it as well, but constant seasickness drew him away. He went to work for the Fish, Food and Allied Workers Union as a union rep. Because he understood the fisheries so well, he ended up working for Brian Tobin when Brian was federal minister of Fisheries and Oceans. I believe Brian would say that Max Short was the best and most frank adviser he ever had. Max would tell you what you needed to know, which was not always what you wished to hear.

After Tobin left to become premier, Max stayed on working with other federal Fisheries ministers. We became political allies and personal friends. We spent many long nights, either at his house or mine, talking fisheries and politics and playing cards. We had to buy a new table because of Max's knuckles hitting the table when he had the right card. Max was all about the ordinary working people, and whatever issue might arise in the fishery, he came down on the side of the little guy. Never was this more evident than when a dispute over shrimp prices erupted in the late summer and fall of 2001.

Premier Grimes asked me, in my role as deputy premier, to work with Gerry Reid, minister of Fisheries, to try to settle it. Max Short was part of the team. It was a terrible wrangle. The fishermen wouldn't fish for the prices offered, and as the season dwindled down, the price did not rise.

We had a meeting with the processors' association, and one of the demands was that the provincial government put plant quotas in place. Our response was that they had the shrimp at their disposal and that they should, as a group, make a business decision—an economic decision—on where it should be processed.

The season wore on, and Max pointed out to everyone that not only would the processors and harvesters suffer if the season ran out, but the plant workers would have no income, either—and they were not really a part of the dispute.

Max and I were both living in the Goulds at the time this problem was dragging on. Each morning during this dispute, we drove to work together, using this extra undisturbed time to try to find a successful solution to the problem. Max kept at me with, "You've got to get this done today!"

I was so frustrated one morning when he was driving, I told him, "I'm concerned, too, about all the people who will have no income, but we're not going to be run roughshod over by the other side!" Max claims that I pounded the dash so hard with my fist in making my point that it left a permanent dent in what had been an unblemished new car.

Eventually, we reached an agreement, and Max got his wish to see the harvesters and the fish plant workers with enough income to get through the winter. Max, now in his eighties, is still a man of the people and has their best interests at heart.

Afterword

No doubt I've missed a few politicians of whom I should have spoken. There are also many more stories which I could have told as well, thousands of other people I should have thanked. Perhaps I will do that in volume two!

Writing this book has been a cathartic experience for me. While reliving the past seventy-some years through this exercise, I have come to realize how blessed I have been, how much I owe to so many—my Maker, my parents, my family, my upbringing in Ladle Cove, and the dear people of the Fogo and Bonavista North districts.

* * * * *

I love my kids very much and am proud of all three of them. The one regret that I have about life (and in particular my later involvement in politics) is the amount of time I spent away from my three children: Cynthia, Christine, and Conrad. As hard as it was at times being a politician, it must have been just as hard or harder being the child of one. I see that now, in retrospect. I wish I had understood it better then.

In speaking with Christine recently, she talked about the time that I lost in my campaign for a seat in the 1989 election. She was only sixteen at the time, and she was teased, harassed, and even physically attacked. No doubt in the political fervour of the 1990s, all three of them had to face the same thing.

Fortunately, though, she and her sister and brother came through their childhood remarkably well. All three avoided many of the ills that modern society inflicted on some of their peers.

I remember when Cynthia was about nine or ten years old, she had a little dog that got run over on the road, and she was broken-hearted over it. I bought her a beautiful little chestnut Newfoundland pony—a couple of hands taller than June, the pony of my childhood. His name was Charlie. We built a small barn and corral for the pony, and she looked after him. I bought her a saddle and had sleighs made for her.

The kids at school started teasing her that they were going to let him out of the barn. A girl that age having her own horse was rare—and you know what kids can be like. One day after school, Cynthia went missing. We didn't know where she had gone. We were scared to death.

Finally, we found her over in the barn with the doors barred. She had a lunch packed. She was with a new little dog that we had—and a big pitchfork. She was going to stay there all night, and, in her words, "They dare not come in through that door to let my horse out!"

At the time she wanted to become a veterinarian. She is now a clinical pharmacist in Ottawa Civic Hospital. She's married and has two kids, Ryan and Nicole, now teenagers.

My other daughter, Christine, was born August 16, 1973, just before I went back to university to get my master's. She is an electrical engineer and worked for the federal government. She's on a leave of absence now and doing her master's in psychology. I tell her, jokingly, that if she would use me as a subject and can analyze my psyche, she would be a genius. She's married and has a son by the name of Jeremy, and she lives in Ottawa. An excellent student, as was Cynthia, and if she doesn't get high nineties in a course, she thinks she's done terribly.

So far I have three grandchildren, the apples of my eye: Ryan, Jeremy, and Nicole.

My third child, Conrad, was born a few years later, on April 16, 1981. He works as an advanced paramedic and respiratory technologist with ORNGE. (It used to be called Ontario Air Ambulance Services Company—OAASC. Its name was changed in 2006 to better relate to the distinct orange colour of its airplanes and ground vehicles.) Conrad is thirty-five now, and his empathy with the patients and the love he has for his work are a joy to see.

My children live in Ottawa, so they are all there together, and that's good. The only bad thing is I don't get to see them enough. I get up there as often as I can. I see some of what I missed, now, as I watch my grandkids grow.

Young people often enter politics with the goal of making a difference in the lives of those in their community. That, in my opinion, is a fine ideal to pursue. I would encourage them to do so, but I urge them not to neglect the most precious things in life: their very own children. You can't go back and be there for them when their crises have passed.

As I write this, both of my daughters and their three kids are visiting Dora and me. I asked the kids for a few memories that they might have which I could include in this book. I also spoke to a couple of other close family members. What follows is their commentary and their memories about growing up.

Dr. Bert Tulk, the son of my uncle Beaton, and my first cousin

My father, after whom Beaton was named, died at a young age. I still

Bert Tulk

have a letter he wrote in 1944, from the Netherlands, during the Second World War. He was proud to hear that Beaton was named after him and would have been even prouder, after his untimely death in 1966, if he could have lived to see how Beaton was there to support his family. After my dad died, Mom would not sell his truck—but she sold his 1960 Chevrolet to Beaton, who remained close and available whenever we needed him.

Beaton helped us with our home improvements, maintenance, and transportation, and he served as a mentor and adviser to me. I made my first trip to St. John's with Beaton in 1968 when I was twelve years old—a major event in the life of an outport Newfoundland boy. Listening to Beaton talk about classic literature, social injustice, and politics made a profound impression on my young mind.

Another indelible memory is of Beaton at the wheel of that big truck—I'm sure we looked like the Beverley Hillbillies going to California—hauling all my family's belongings when we made the move to St. John's in 1975. Just another example, among many, of Beaton being there in times of need.

Beaton, of course, became a popular teacher and school administrator. He introduced the great bard, Shakespeare, to a whole generation in our bay. "The stage" took on a second meaning to those of us whose only definition had been "a place to process fish."

While still in education, he successfully lobbied for roads, schools, and recreational facilities for our rural area. Even at a young age he knew the importance of getting to the right people—and he knew who those people were. I remember being part of a delegation of three people, Beaton included, who went to the Confederation Building to negotiate paving in Ladle Cove and Aspen Cove. Beaton insisted on meeting the deputy minister.

We got to see him, too, and the minister found out about the paving equipment being blockaded from leaving by members of our community back home. Our roads got paved. Beaton knew how to use all angles to turn a lost cause into a success. It's no surprise to me that he became successful in politics, ending up as premier. I remember during one of the elections hearing Ed Roberts, on television, remark that Beaton was the most knowledgeable MHA/parliamentarian he knew regarding Rules of the House. Beaton did his homework.

Another memory I have is of listening to game seven of the Canada-Russia series, with Beaton, on the car radio. Beaton, a big hockey fan, was travelling with me from Carmanville to Ladle Cove. That moment when Paul Henderson's winning goal went in the net holds a lot of memories for countless people. I have an additional memory. Beaton punched the dash so hard, he broke it!

His success in education, business, and politics is well-known, but as a cousin—more like a brother—I got to see his private side. He was all about family and helping others—and he still is. Beaton, thanks for everything, bro.

My daughter Christine Tulk
Lessons learned from Dad:

1/ There's not much worse than being a Tory. A Tory is not just someone who votes Conservative—although that's bad enough. A Tory is someone who doesn't help people in need—or someone who thinks that poor, uneducated people are beneath him. Since then I've met a number of people without a university education, and who do not speak "perfect" English, who know a lot more than I do.

2/ Notwithstanding #1 above, getting an education is a big deal. Dad read all the books that came into Ladle Cove and, in between them, read his Bible. Reading is important.

3/ Being lazy is not a good trait. People don't respect those who can but will not work. When I was eight or nine, I wouldn't help harvest the vegetables like my sister, Cynthia, did. At Sunday dinner that week, Dad took out $5 and passed it down to her. He looked at me to signal that I was getting nothing for not contributing.

I also remember watching the adults playing 500s, watching westerns on TV, and Bugs Bunny. I remember Dad telling me that I was a good singer. I remember him making sure that Grandfather knew that I was just as smart as Cynthia. I remember how excited we were—we couldn't wait for him to get home on Friday evening. Mom would get us to clean up and dress up because Dad was on his way home. I was proud of Dad. I guess that's what made me want to do something worthwhile in life, too. I love you, Dad.

Henry, my daughter Christine Tulk, and Jeremy

My daughter Cynthia Waye (Tulk)

My earliest memory I have of Dad is being sent to my room. I think I might have been about four years old. As I recall, some-one had left some small change on a table in our basement, and I had taken it. When Dad asked if I had the money, I denied it. But he was pretty sure I did, so off I went to my room to think about what I had done. I don't think I was there for long, but it was long enough to get the message—honesty is the best policy.

Being a good worker was another value he tried to instill in us kids. Every summer our family planted a big vegetable garden on the land that used to belong to my great-grandparents Frank and Edith West. We usually grew enough potato, carrot, turnip, parsnip, and cabbage to last the whole winter. Every spring we would all go over and plant. My parents did most of the work, but we had our jobs, too. I think I got pretty good at planting spuds after a while. Then there was the weeding, which of course had to be done off and on during the summer. I guess one day I was not enthusiastic about getting the job done. I remember Dad sitting me down to explain that part of the reason we were there was so that when we were older we would know how to work hard. Another good lesson.

My most vivid memory is the day Charlie arrived. It was the summer I turned eleven. All summer, Dad had me drying hay. He would get one of the young men from Ladle Cove to cut the grass, because he didn't want me amputating one of my feet with the scythe. After that, it was up to me. The hay had to be turned twice a day until it was dry. If it rained, I had to jump on my bike, race to whatever field the hay was in, and rake it into piles so it would not get wet. Then when the rain stopped it had to be spread out again. Luckily, I think that was one of Newfoundland's drier summers. Over the summer I made about 3,000 pounds of hay, which all got stored in the barn where we kept our milk cow.

One morning, I was hanging out in our garden with my cousin when I heard a horse neigh. I looked down the road, and there was Dad and Harold West unloading a horse from a trailer. My horse! (Okay, he belonged to Christine, too, but everybody knew he was really mine.) Apparently Dad had gotten sick of hearing me beg for a horse. He told me later that he thought I would get sick of looking after the horse in a couple of months. Joke was on him—I (okay, we) had Charlie for five years.

Also, I remember fishing with a bamboo pole (I never caught anything except leaves), card parties with Dad and his buddies playing 500s, watching the Montreal Canadiens on Saturday nights, and church on Sunday. That about sums Dad up—tell the truth, work hard, but don't forget to have some fun.

John Waye, Nicole, my daughter Cynthia Waye (Tulk), and Ryan

<u>My niece Gay Clarke</u>

I remember a lot of things about Beaton. He was driving the last time I was on a horse-drawn sled. Beaton was on the front sled, holding Charlie's reins. I was hanging on for dear life on the back one. We came flying across Ladle Cove Pond and onto the road, and as we passed Uncle Jake's stage, my sled started sliding toward the store. We missed it by a hair!

I drove with him again, though. We were having an old-fashioned "time" in Ladle Cove. Father Tulk, which is what I called Beaton's dad, had just come home with his brand new car. He tossed the keys to Beaton and asked him to go collect soup and take it to the Orange Lodge. Of course, I was with him, and we had four big pots of soup on board.

Beaton was driving so fast that when we came to take the turn at the Cut Road, we almost lost the lot of it. We survived, unscalded, and got the car back in reasonably good condition. Nobody knew how close we came to ruining the meal . . . and a brand new car.

The last night that Beaton was premier, he was entertaining guests and well-wishers in a suite at the Hotel Newfoundland. I

Me with my neice Gay Clarke

believe he was surprised to see me, but he came right over. I think he wondered why I had come—whether something was wrong. I told him, "I have only one uncle in the world. Tonight he is premier of our great province. I am here to enjoy and remember it."

I knew, though, at a very young age that Beaton would play a big role in my life. He was there in my teenage years when no one else was—listening, guiding, giving me the structured life I would not have had without him. As an adult, his guidance remained. If I needed to know the right thing to do, he was only a phone call away. When my son was born, without any discussion or hesitation, I chose to call him Beaton, after the man I have the most admiration and respect for.

When Beaton entered politics, our lives became even closer. There is no one any prouder of the father figure in their life than I am of Uncle Beaton. Today I am heavily involved in politics because of our relationship—my mentor and friend. Love you.

When I married Dora in 1996, I was happy to say I inherited her family as well. Samantha, her granddaughter, came to live with us at an early age. She wanted to send her best. She calls me "Pop."

Samantha Callahan, Dora's granddaughter

Pop, there is no combination of words that can describe how grateful I am to have you in my life. There is not enough paper in the world to begin to express how much you mean to me. From day one, you took me into your home and into your heart. You have taught me many life lessons in the past twenty-eight years, but the most important one to me is your unconditional love. Through the ups and downs and everything in between, you have been my number one supporter. And just as you are my number one supporter, I am your number one fan. You inspire me every single day to be better and to do better. To know your worth and to reach for the stars. The impact you've made in my life means the world to me. And what makes my heart *really* full is getting to watch Jayda make her own memories with Grandpa. We love you more than you will ever know!

Kerry-Lynn Callahan, Dora's daughter

Words really cannot express the impact Beaton has had on my life. Beaton has always been a safe outlet for me. He has always been my voice of reason to see through the fog, by being open-minded and willing to listen. He has taught me to be honest, reliable, and work hard no matter what the job. Because he has shown me that he cares, he has always inspired me to work harder and be a better person.

I have watched over the years how he cares about the people around him. No matter if it is his family, friends, colleagues, or constituents, he has helped many people. Whether it is him opening up his home to people in need of a place to stay in town for medical appointments or emergencies, or answering phone calls in the middle of the night for someone who needs his help. Even just wanting an ear.

I have watched him stand his ground for something he believes in. No matter what public opinion or perception, you can be guaranteed he will do what is right.

I admire and respect who he is as a person. I am so proud that Beaton is in my life, that I got to call him family.

I love you, Beaton.

Alicia, Dora's oldest daughter

I grew up surrounded by politicians and journalists. Although I am not a very social person (ask anyone who knows me), it always fascinated me to watch from the sidelines. I have never been involved in either profession, but my unique position has taught me a lot about the importance of good, strong leaders in positions of power, balanced reporting of facts, questioning policies, an educated electorate, and public service.

I have known Beaton Tulk since I was a young girl. He has always been larger than life, at over six feet with his booming voice, and yet even as that young girl, I always felt comfortable around him. Watching him through my own personal microscope has been interesting throughout the years. The man that most people knew from his public persona, I knew through his relationship with my mother.

I had a chance to join Mom and Beaton during one of the election cycles. The night of the election, they had a get-together at the town hall. He lost that night, and I know they were disappointed, but the thing that stands out the most to me is watching them dance . . . just the way they looked at each other, as if they were each other's whole world. That look between them is what a person looks for their whole life, and for that reason, that look, above all other things, makes me appreciate him the most.

A couple of things have always stood out with Beaton. One is his ability to relate to anyone that he comes into contact with. His questions always start with, "What's your last name?" "You are from (insert town name here)?" and, "Who's your father? He works or worked at (name of employer here) and his brother used to fish." Or, "Your mother came from (town name) originally. I knew her sister." And he was always interested. I, the most geographically inept person ever, have always been agog over his knowledge of names, places, and accents. I guess that is why he was in politics and I am not.

Another thing would be how knowledgeable he is. I have attempted to debate him a few times over the years, but I have learned that you don't try to debate him unless you really, really know what you are talking about. You can have your opinion, but make sure you know your facts. If you don't, you will by the time you are finished talking to him.

Lastly, never least, about his kids. The look of pride in his eyes when he talks about his children and grandchildren. That is what this book is about. It is a window into his life in politics, and he wants his family to see and know this about him. When we were all growing up, none of us really knew what he did or how he did it. It was politics. This gives his family a taste of the man that the public saw and gives the public a taste of who this man is as a person.

When Beaton was in politics, I couldn't wait for the day that he would get out. Politics is not just about the politician, but it envelops the politician's family as well. Over the years, however, I have learned how much he lives and breathes politics. He loves it. He loves the challenge. He loves being part of the government. He loves meeting people, and he loves helping people. He loves this province. He has dedicated his career to helping define what he thought would be most beneficial to this province and its people. He would work his hardest to ensure that this province was not left out and received what it was entitled to. Politics, in its most positive definition, is a big part of Beaton Tulk.

My son, Conrad Tulk

Some of my best memories with Dad are of us travelling together, and travelling to see a Montreal Canadiens game was one of my most unforgettable trips. Dad had gotten us tickets at the Montreal Forum to see the Canadiens play the Pittsburgh Penguins. We sat in the lower level, behind Patrick Roy. Dad said that each team had secured their respective spots in the playoffs and the outcome of the game didn't matter, but the game was still incredible—we even got to watch Mario Lemieux play one or two shifts. Montreal won the game 9-1!

While watching hockey was exciting, travelling to Montreal was not the most eventful trip we had together. When returning from one of our trips to Nova Scotia, we were taking an Air Atlantic Dash-8 flight from Halifax to Newfoundland. Shortly after takeoff, the aircraft suffered an engine failure that required a quick return to Halifax. I don't remember Dad being particularly upset during the twenty minutes it took us to get back to the airport, but I do remember, a few years later, he did say he wasn't able to fall asleep on an airplane quite as easily following that flight. Given my career as a flight paramedic, I hope it will be the first—and last—in-flight emergency I experience. I usually flew on standby when I travelled with Dad, and on another Dash-8 flight there were no seats available in the back of the plane, and I was able to sit in the jump seat. Dad offered his seat to me, but I was more than happy to see the view from the front.

Other happy memories include fishing trips we took together. I caught my first (and only) salmon on the Gander River, despite an earlier fishing trip to Labrador where we were guaranteed to fill our licence.

One piece of advice Dad gave me has stuck with me through the years: do your best at whatever you decide to do, no matter what it is. I became a primary care paramedic, then returned to college to get a diploma in respiratory therapy. After several years practising as an RT, I ultimately decided to return to pre-hospital care and upgraded my paramedicine certificate to become an advanced care paramedic. I never felt pressure from Dad to pick one career over another as long as I was happy with what I did, and he never discouraged me from going back to school to further my education. I love my job as a flight paramedic, and I strive to be the best at what I do—just like Dad always told me.

Amelia and my son, Conrad Tulk

I want to say that when we lost that engine and had to return to Halifax for a few seconds, the airplane went into a forty-five-degree dive, and it took the pilot about fifteen or twenty seconds to get it under control. Conrad was about eight years old. To assure him that everything was okay, I reminded him that when I went duck hunting in my boat with *two* engines, I often had one break down and come to land with the other. As quick as a wink, he replied, "Yes, but Dad, you had water under your boat."

I have often had a good laugh at the wit of that eight-year-old. And, by the way, I was scared, but fathers don't show fear to their sons in that kind of situation.

Born in Ladle Cove, Newfoundland and Labrador, Beaton Tulk resides in Musgravetown with his wife, Dora. He graduated from Memorial University with bachelor of arts, bachelor of education, and master's of eductional administration degrees. He also later obtained a Canadian securities investment diploma. Beaton was a supervising principal for the Carmanville school system from 1974 to 1979. He was first elected to the Newfoundland House of Assembly in 1979 as the Liberal Party member for Fogo and was re-elected in 1982 and 1985. While in provincial politics, he served as deputy minister of Children and Youth Services, and later minister of both Forest Resources and Agrifoods and the Department of Development and Rural Renewal. In 2000, he became the seventh premier of Newfoundland and Labrador when his predecessor, Brian Tobin, left provincial politics to run federally.

Laurie Blackwood Pike, a.k.a. Grandpa Pike, was born in Stanhope, Newfoundland and Labrador. He is retired from his position as business development manager with a national chain of hardware and building supply stores. In 2017, he received the Estwing Gold Hammer Award—the industry's recognition for his contributions. In 1986, he bought a rural general store, developed a logo, and branded the business "Grandpa Pike's." His unique store was profiled in the hardware industry's *Hardware Merchandising* magazine. In recent years, Grandpa Pike has used his nickname for charity work. In 2007, he partnered with the Children's Wish Foundation of Canada, Newfoundland & Labrador Chapter, to release a music CD. In 2009, he partnered with them again to produce a gospel Christmas CD. He is married to Kathleen Pike and has one daughter, Laurie Shannon. *A Man of My Word* is his second book. His first book, *Grandpa Pike's Outhouse Reader*, has appeared in *Atlantic Books Today*'s bestsellers lists.

Members of the House of Assembly Who Served During My Tenure*

A. Brian Peckford
Alec Snow
Alvin Hewlett
Anna Thistle
Anthony Sparrow
Art Reid
Bill Ramsay
Bob French
Brian Tobin
Bud Hulan
Calvin Mitchell
Charles Brett
Charles Power
Chris Decker
Chuck Furey
Clyde Wells
Danny Dumaresque
Dave Gilbert
Derrick Hancock
Don Whalen
Donald C. Hollett
Donald C. Jamieson
Donald Stewart
E. Douglas Oldford
Eddie Joyce
Edward J. Byrne
Edward M. Roberts
Eric Gullage
Ernest McLean
Eugene Hiscock
Everett K. Osmond
Fabian G. Manning
Frederick B. Rowe
Frederick Stagg
Freeman White
Garfield Warren
Gary Vey

Gene Long
Gerald Ottenheimer
Gerald Smith
Gerry Reid
Glen Tobin
Glenn C. Greening
Graham Flight
H. Neil Windsor
Haig Young
Harold Andrews
Harold Barrett
Harold D. Andrews
Harvey Hodder
Hazel R. Newhook
Hubert Kitchen
Hugh Twomey
Ida M. Reid
Jack Byrne
Jack Harris
James C. Morgan
James G. Reid
James Hodder
James Russell
Jerome Dinn
Jim Kelland
Jim Walsh
Joan Marie Aylward
John A. Carter
John Butt
John Collins
John Crane
John Efford
John McLennon
John Ottenheimer
Joseph Goudie
Judy M. Foote
Julie Bettney

K. George Sweeney
Kay Young
Kelvin Parsons
Kevin Aylward
Kevin Parsons
Len Stirling
Leo Barry
Leonard Simms
Leslie R. Thoms
Lloyd G. Matthews
Lloyd Snow
Loyola Hearn
Loyola Sullivan
Luke Woodrow
Lynn E. Verge
Mary Hodder
Melvin Penney
Mike Mackey
Milton Peach
Nick Careen
Norman Doyle
Oliver Langdon
Patrick McNicholas
Patt Cowan
Paul Dicks
Paul Shelley
Percy Barrett
Perry Canning
Peter Fenwick
Peter J. Walsh
Ralph Wiseman
Randy Collins
Randy W. Collins
Ray Hunter
Raymond Baird
Rex Gibbons
Rick Woodford

Robert Aylward
Robert Mercer
Rod Moores
Roger Fitzgerald
Roger Grimes
Roger Simmons
Ronald Dawe
Ross Wiseman
Sandra C. Kelly
Sheila Osborne
Stephen A. Neary
Ted A. Blanchard
Thomas G. Rideout
Thomas Murphy
Thomas V. Hickey
Tom Hedderson
Tom Lush
Tom Osborne
Trevor Bennett
Trevor Taylor
Wallace House
Wallace Young
Wally Andersen
Walter C. Carter
Walter G. Cross
Walter Noel
William Andersen III
William J. Patterson
William Marshall
William Matthews
William N. Rowe
William Ramsay
Wilson E. Callan
Winston Baker
Yvonne J. Jones

*The lessons I learned from them all were numerous. The members of this microcosm of Newfoundland and Labrador were people who wanted to serve their province as opposed to themselves.

Index